T0339466

AN HISTORICAL ASSESSMENT OF LEADERSHIP IN TURBULENT TIMES

This unique book provides lessons on how to effect good leadership in turbulent times by taking a historical lens and examining the life and impact of Clovis I, king of the Franks. Through the exploration of how this individual managed the unstable times where so many others had failed, the book provides an original take on leadership, focusing on the ways we can learn from and be inspired by his history.

This book offers an insightful and detailed case study of Clovis I, as it explores his struggles and triumphs in the face of turbulent times. The book presents implications for students of leadership today and examines why the story of Clovis I reveals the salience of leadership during times of uncertainty and change. Ultimately, the author foresees the rise of myriad leaders trying to manage the upheaval in the twenty-first century, with the likelihood that somebody like Clovis I will emerge, pursuing ambition and reordering civilization on a colossal scale, leaving a legacy that will endure for a further thousand years.

This book will be of interest to leadership and history scholars and advanced students in leadership studies.

Nathan W. Harter has taught leadership studies since 1989, when he began teaching at Purdue University in West Lafayette, Indiana. Today, he teaches at Christopher Newport University in Newport News, Virginia. He is the author of several books and numerous articles and book chapters on leadership.

AN HISTORICAL ASSESSMENT OF LEADERSHIP IN TURBULENT TIMES

Lessons Learned from Clovis I, King of the Franks

Nathan W. Harter

Routledge
Taylor & Francis Group

NEW YORK AND LONDON

Cover image: © Getty Images

First published 2023
by Routledge
605 Third Avenue, New York, NY 10158

and by Routledge
4 Park Square, Milton Park, Abingdon, Oxon, OX14 4RN

Routledge is an imprint of the Taylor & Francis Group, an informa business

© 2023 Nathan W. Harter

Library of Congress Cataloging-in-Publication Data
Names: Harter, Nathan, author. Title: An historical assessment of
   leadership in turbulent times : lessons learned from Clovis I, King of
   the Franks / Nathan W. Harter.
Description: New York : Routledge, 2023. | Includes bibliographical
   references and index. |
Identifiers: LCCN 2022030631 (print) | LCCN 2022030632 (ebook) |
   ISBN 9781032286440 (hardback) | ISBN 9781032278957 (paperback) |
   ISBN 9781003297802 (ebook)
Subjects: LCSH: Clovis, King of the Franks, approximately 466-511. |
   Clovis, King of the Franks, approximately 466-511—Influence. |
   Leadership—Philosophy. | Charisma (Personality trait) | France—
   History—To 987. | France—Church history—To 987.
Classification: LCC DC67 .H37 2023 (print) | LCC DC67 (ebook) |
   DDC 944/.01—dc23/eng/20220720
LC record available at https://lccn.loc.gov/2022030631
LC ebook record available at https://lccn.loc.gov/2022030632

ISBN: 978-1-032-28644-0 (hbk)
ISBN: 978-1-032-27895-7 (pbk)
ISBN: 978-1-003-29780-2 (ebk)

DOI: 10.4324/9781003297802

Typeset in Bembo
by Apex CoVantage, LLC

To my colleagues at Christopher Newport University, who must now manage the routinization of charisma.

CONTENTS

ACKNOWLEDGMENTS

This project began during the pandemic of 2020. I must thank the library staff at my university, especially Jesse Spencer, for providing many of the materials on which this manuscript relies. Furthermore, I have been buoyed throughout by the friendship here of Robert Colvin, Brent Cusher, and William Donaldson. I appreciated Christina Chronister's upbeat manner at Routledge, who passed me off seamlessly to Emilie Coin, Zoe Thomson, and Maddie Gray. The following persons have contributed to my grasp of the content, even if the ultimate responsibility for what appears in these pages is entirely mine: Adrianna de Santis, Eli Goossens, Lia Sternizki, and the charismatic exemplar Paul Trible.

In all things, I give to God the glory. And to Karin, my long-suffering wife and best friend, I give my whole heart daily.

INTRODUCTION

Students of leadership who find themselves living through turbulent times ought to gain critical distance from their own circumstances and consider successful leadership from another place and time. One way to learn leadership is through historical lenses, where evidence accrues as to what worked and what did not. The tribulations of the present can often resemble previous epochs. And although one cannot always consult the past for specific answers to problems in the present, the recorded examples of leadership may suggest pathways forward and inspire leaders today to equivalent exertions.

This book opens with an anecdote written over a thousand years ago about a young chieftain of a small tribe faced with trials and opportunities on a grand scale. Here was a teenager on the verge of colossal change. Subsequent sections will hearken back to this little story as a kind of allegory. What follows the anecdote is a fairly typical case study in Chapter 1 about the leader depicted in the story, a man who came to be known as Clovis I, king of the Franks. Immediately after the case study about Clovis, Chapter 2 takes up the topic of charisma. Chapter 3 examines leadership at lower levels in the social hierarchy, distributed throughout the regime over which Clovis had to preside and on which he was required to depend. These attempts to govern various localities provide the social context within which his own leadership should be understood. Then Chapter 4 considers the broader historical context about the fall of the Roman Empire, the immigration of barbarians, and the rise of the Catholic Church, revealing the tendency of historians to interpret the reign of Clovis differently depending on their peculiar lenses. One unexpected lens does suggest itself: namely, the Renaissance study of leadership known as *The Prince* conducted by Niccolò Machiavelli. This section of my book asks the following question: to what extent does Clovis of the Franks exemplify Machiavelli's infamous prince? Finally, before alluding to a number of implications for students of leadership today, Chapter 5 examines why the example of Clovis reveals the salience of leadership during times of uncertainty and change. A map of Gaul and a time line of his life appear as appendices.

It is my contention that one of the purposes of leadership studies is to populate the imagination, contributing exemplars, regardless of whether the attentive student goes on from there to lead, follow, or remain (as I am) a student of social dynamics, presuming to judge the times through which they happen to be living.

Originally, I had thought it would be unnecessary to explain the value of studying history, especially for understanding leadership. Certainly, I am not a credentialed historian. Instead, I might label myself an enthusiastic consumer. To my mind, any question about the value of history was settled by many of the founders of this field of inquiry, including James MacGregor Burns, Tom Wren, and Suze Wilson. To my dismay, however, an anonymous reviewer for a leadership conference who was asked to assess a case study about someone from antiquity rejected the proposal, asking rhetorically what history has to do with the present. Another reviewer for the same proposal rejected it because "it sounds too much like a story."

Far be it from me in these pages to defend the uses of history. Nothing I say can counter such ignorance. To sweep aside so brusquely mountains of evidence and generations of scholarship as these anonymous reviewers did does the profession no credit. I mention it only to share the revelation that apparently not everyone accepts the testimony of the ages. A critic is certainly entitled to question my methods and conclusions. That would be a conversation devoutly to be wished. It is just that I see no merit in a fruitless squabble over the abstract virtues of history for the study of leadership.

Indeed, from the outset, let me make my purpose plain. I believe that, in many important respects, the present through which we are living in the twenty-first century resembles the time period to be encountered in these pages. I am not so naïve as to think that the two epochs are identical. That would be a foolish assertion. Neither will I argue that what we need today is precisely the kind of leadership practiced thousands of years ago in a completely different context. The differences are many and profound, incalculable. That does not preclude us from learning things of present utility, for the dynamics we find throughout history suggest parallels between that time and this.

Each is a period of transition, which I call a liminal state or condition, not in small things, but in profound ways. We are undergoing a shift of enormous proportions in the year 2022. It is only an optical illusion (or a lack of courage) to believe otherwise. Looking back at similar epochs, we find that some of their practices succeeded and some failed. Part of the world persisted and even flourished, whereas other parts dwindled and completely vanished. How they managed the challenges will be instructive, and the tools we use today to analyze their experience can be used (with minor adaptations) to analyze our own. And the investigation begins with a question, noted by José Ortega y Gasset: "What then happens in a society – and what in particular happened in Rome – after the loss of a firm and common belief in matters of leadership" (1940/1946, p. 22)?

Ultimately, yes, I foresee the rise of myriad leaders trying to manage the upheaval in the twenty-first century, with the likelihood that somebody like Clovis I will emerge, pursuing ambition and reordering civilization on a colossal scale, leaving a legacy that will endure for a thousand years. The possibility is neither a good thing nor a bad thing. Or should I say that it will be both? To the extent that we can participate in that emergence, whether to encourage or discourage it, then let the story of Clovis guide us in our selections, so that we might exploit what is good and limit what is bad during the days to come – and not just let things happen around us, as though we have nothing to say.

It would be folly to pretend that I can peer over the far horizon and guess what form the future will take. Nobody stood on the ramparts along the Rhine in 400 CE shouting, "Here comes feudalism!" It is not given to us to know what comes next. The moment requires our participation to be sure, together, in order to influence the direction that civilization takes. And quite possibly, walking among us already is a personage the stature of Clovis. We should probably ask ourselves: "And what rough beast, its hour come round at last,/Slouches towards Bethlehem to be born?" Or, given the alternate ethos of democracy that we ostensibly enjoy, is there a way to cope with liminality in our context *without* relying on such an outsized personage?

Reference

Ortega y Gasset, J. (1940/1946). *Concord and liberty* (H. Weyl, trans.). W. W. Norton & Co.

THE FABLED VASE OF SOISSONS

From *History of the Franks*, written by Gregory Bishop of Tours in 594 CE (1973, p. 37f), the story is told of a ceremony among the Franks to divide the spoils after a battle. This was early in the career of Clovis, who was at the time still a teenager. Among the items was a large and beautiful vase that had belonged to the local church, and Clovis as the chief asked his men to let him return it. One soldier insisted that the young chief had no right to make any such exception. Instead, the soldier took his battle-ax and shattered the vase so that nobody could have it. Clovis acknowledged that their tradition did not allow for such an exception to be made, so he held his peace. A year later, however, Clovis assembled the soldiers for inspection, and upon coming to the man who had broken the vase the year before, Clovis took his own battle-ax and split the man's skull (de Bonnechose, 1856, p. 15). *Sic transit more.*

Notice what is happening. Clovis as warlord is trying to take one vase more than was his due. When a subordinate called him to account publicly and even destroyed that vase in righteous indignation, Clovis acquiesced, for that had been the custom. Nothing further was said. The subordinate was technically correct, based on tribal tradition. Yet something had most definitely changed.

This anecdote, which according to Michel Foucault would have been familiar to every French schoolboy (1997, p. 150), reveals something profound about the changing role of leadership under that young barbarian chieftain named Clovis. Foucault identified this moment in fact as the tipping point, the historical bifurcation from Late Antiquity to the Early Middle Ages (1997, p. 153).[1] So it would

---

1 Foucault argues that Germanic law (as he called it) was based on the struggle between the aggrieved and the alleged culprit, an ordeal left for no third party to adjudicate. In other terms,

be reasonable to ask, who was Clovis? And what was going on in Gaul at the time of his rise to power? Finally, what might be a few of the lessons regarding leadership today? The story is vivid. Will it teach us very much?

References

de Bonnechose, E. (1856). *History of France: From the invasion of the Franks under Clovis, to the accession of Louis Philippe* (2nd ed., W. Robson, trans.). Routledge.

Elden, S. (2017). *Foucault: The birth of power*. Polity.

Foucault, M. (1997). *"Society must be defended": Lectures at the College de France, 1975–76* (D. Macey, trans.). Picador.

Foucault, M. (1977). *Discipline and punish: The birth of the prison* (A. Sheridan, trans.). Vintage.

Gregory Bishop of Tours. (594/1973). *History of the Franks* (E. Brehaut, trans.). Octagon Books.

---

the outcome would be reached by means of violence between the interested parties, where might makes right (Elden, 2017, p. 61, citing Foucault, 2015). Only later would the power of a sovereign to punish evolve toward reforms and the administrative state (Elden, 2017, p. 141; see generally Foucault, 1977). Thus, it would be anachronistic to expect Clovis to adhere to practices that did not prevail until much more recently.

1

ABOUT THE LEADERSHIP OF CLOVIS, KING OF THE FRANKS

The days of the Roman Empire were coming to an end.

After Julius Caesar had subdued the territory we know today as France and returned to Rome in 50 BCE, the conquered people found themselves under Roman rule and tutelage for about five centuries, at which point the empire began to collapse (Pufendorf, 1695/2013, p. 191f). During this imperial twilight, Gaul was populated by a variety of tribes, including the indigenous Galli, Roman settlers, transient Goths, Vandals, Burgundians, and so on, including a barbarian people of little note who had crossed into Gaul and enjoyed an ambivalent relationship with the dwindling authority of the empire on its easternmost frontier. Romans called them Franks, but in truth they were a loose affiliation or tribal union of separate peoples from along the Rhineland (Innes, 2004, p. 170; see Wood, 2013, p. 22, citing de Boulainvilliers, 1727).[1] Susan Wise Bauer calls them a confederation (2010, p. 173). John Riddle is more prosaic, calling them "a tribal swarm" (2016, p. 80). J.M. Wallace-Hadrill puts it sardonically, saying that the Franks enjoyed "less than an occasional sense of unity" (1962, p. 67). Patrick Geary uses a metaphor, saying that for generations tribal membership had been fluid (1988, p. 53). With Clovis, we can witness what Geary called the "ethnogenesis" of the Franks as a people.[2]

---

1 The meaning of the term "Franks" is unclear. It is even unclear whether it was a term they would have used about themselves. To a great extent, it would have been an identity given to these people by outsiders who needed a label (Reimitz, 2019, ch. 3). Clovis himself appears to have avoided referring to himself as king of the Franks because he saw himself as the king of all peoples within his domain and not just of his ethnic confreres (see, e.g., Geary, 1988, p. 90).
2 Peter Heather (2006) refers to this period as the formation of supergroups, alliances among kinsmen that have come to be known as tribes such as the Goths, Burgundians, and Vandals (pp. 450–459).

DOI: 10.4324/9781003297802-1

Probably the most obvious division among the Franks pertained to their land of origin. The Ripuarian Franks lived along the rivers; the Salian (or salty) Franks lived on the seacoast. It was the Salian Franks who made periodic incursions into Roman-held Gaul. The Ripuarian Franks would follow later (cf. Graceffa, 2022, p. 67).

After years trying to displace these long-haired "Franks" and repulse their periodic incursions, Rome had decided around 287 CE to invite them to settle the frontier along the Rhine as a buffer against a greater menace to the east. That is, they co-opted their enemies by offering the Franks land in Gaul and an introduction to Roman norms and standards (Pufendorf, 1695/2013, p. 193).[3] Why would they do this? During that era, Attila the Hun and his successors were driving entire peoples westward, including the Goths, who needed somewhere to go.[4] According to Ian Wood (2013), this period in history has gone by different names, e.g., *la tournamente des invasions*, denoting hostile motives (p. 285); the Migration Period, denoting a demographic shift (p. 298); and, in a more neutral cast, simply a "Transformation of the Roman World" (p. 315ff; see generally Wood, 2017).[5] Thus began an uneasy truce between a waning empire (Rome) and these fractious border tribes (the Franks), during which the Franks learned Roman ways (Drinkwater, 2007, p. 348).[6] It would be a misnomer to call the Franks conquerors. They were more like displaced refugees

---

Scattered little clans beyond the border unified and consolidated in response to both the Roman and the Hunnic empires, partly out of self-defense, but also as a way of organizing themselves for purposes of trade. Thus, it would be misleading, in his opinion, to regard the Franks as some kind of preexisting tribe just beyond the borders. On the concept of ethnogenesis and the Franks, see generally Graceffa, 2022, p. 68f citing Reinhard Wenskus.

3 It would be a misnomer to call this phase a "conquest" (Wood, 2013, p. 182). These Franks were invited and consequently blended into the Roman system. One author points out that, instead of displacing the Romans, the Franks sought to perpetuate the empire (see Wood, 2013, p. 312) – that is, they saw their increasing involvement as part of the renewal of the empire. By the time of Clovis, they had been part of the empire for some time (Mathisen, 2019).

4 Walter Goffart (2006) rejects this hypothesis, not because it is mistaken, but because it is not supported by the evidence (see, e.g., p. 18; contra Heather, 2006, pp. 167, 361, & 433).

5 Much depends on whether one is viewing these events as the fate of the empire from Rome's perspective or as the saga of the Germanic peoples settling in western Europe (Wood, 2013, pp. 1, 76, & 312). In fact, writes Wood (2013), ultimately one can adopt some combination of *three different* perspectives: the fall of the Roman Empire, a history of the barbarian migration (known as the *Völkerwanderung*), and the rise of the Christian (Catholic) church in Western Europe. All three movements converged.

6 In its last days, Rome had difficulty recruiting a sufficient number of soldiers, and so as a way of maintaining its supply, it relied increasingly on non-Romans to serve (Mathisen, 2019; Wood, 2013, p. 9; Geary, 1988, p. 21). Off and on, Franks had served in the Roman army since the time of Julius Caesar, supplying a number of successful commanders. It was not unusual for a fighting man to leave his family, go serve Rome, and then return with Roman artifacts that would be buried with him as a sign of respect for his years of service (Halsall, 2014, p. 525). This knowledge of Roman methods obtained by the Franks would prove advantageous later against the less-sophisticated tactics of the other so-called barbarians (see Laing, 2000).

(Wallace-Hadrill, 1962, p. 9).[7] What took shape over the years was a "client king-dom" that belonged to the Roman world, where the Franks enjoyed "reciprocal, if unequal, relations at every level" (Heather, 2006, p. 83f).

With increasing pressure from migrating war parties to the east and a power vacuum to the west as Rome imploded, the Franks expanded into Gaul under the leadership of the Merovingian rulers, beginning with Childeric (456–82 CE).[8] Clovis was Childeric's son. Each of them, Childeric and Clovis, was able to establish himself as ostensibly favored by the Roman *imperium*, which still had some residual status (Daly, 1994, p. 624). More importantly, Clovis (who is sometimes referred to as Clotwig, Clouis, Chlodovic, Chlodovicus, and Chlo-dowech) would convert to Roman Catholicism, thereby securing the favor of the institutional church and the believers throughout Gaul, to stand against pagans and heretics alike.

In a manner of speaking, the Franks became a hybrid or synthesis of two peo-ples, such that over time they capitalized on features of each.[9] The Romans influ-enced the Franks along the border, and the Franks influenced the Romans – even before any formal mingling (Geary, 1988, pp. 58 & 86). Historians sometimes call theirs a Gallo-Roman society (Daly, 1994, p. 623); yet this label overlooks the distinctly foreign character of the original Franks (Pufendorf, 1695/2013, p. 192). Among scholars, the process of integration now goes by the ungainly label of "mischzivilisation" (Drinkwater, 2007, p. 349; see also Ruckert, 2011), a term translated into English as "a mixed civilization." The Franks, hoping to invoke a remote kinship with the Romans, emphasized their common ancestry dating all the way back to the legend of Troy, claiming to have fled from that defeated city – albeit in different directions (e.g., Graceffa, 2022, p. 55, citing Fredegar III; Geary, 1988, p. 77f; cf. Goffart, 2006). Ian Wood (2013) quotes a nineteenth century author named Alessandro Manzoni (1847) as follows:

> Two peoples living in the same country, divided by name, language, clothing, interests, and, in part, laws: such was the state in which for an

---

7 Guy Halsall (2014) questions this narrative, arguing that the various "Germanic" tribes came and went across the border repeatedly over the years, without the motive of fleeing some invading horde. The so-called domino theory, in which one tribe pushes the next tribe westward, which in turn pushes the next tribe westward even further west, will not suffice (p. 529). Ralph Mathisen (2019) concurs.

8 The Merovingian dynasty was named for an ancestor of Clovis named Meroveus (or Sea-Fighter), who according to legend had aided Rome in its initial repulse of Attila the Hun (Wallace-Hadrill, 1962, p. 70). The actual existence of a person named Meroveus is regrettably in doubt.

9 Raymond van Dam (1985) writes: "In contrast with other barbarian kingdoms, Romans and Franks were free to intermarry, and they did so with apparently little tension" (p. 179). He does not mention the nature of the corresponding relationship with the indigenous people. By the seventh century, regardless, the people of every ethnicity in the region regarded themselves not as Roman but as Frankish (Ward-Perkins, 2005, p. 78; see also p. 80).

undefined and indefinable time, almost the whole of Europe found itself, after the invasions and settlements of the barbarians.

(p. 115)

For many reasons, one might label the conditions throughout Gaul as distinctly liminal, a term that will be examined more closely later.

Guy Halsall (2014) goes one step further, pointing out that it would be an error to lump everyone beyond the border into one unit of analysis with a single label. The binary characterization of Roman, on the one side, and barbarian, on the other side, is a myth. The only reason we might call those beyond the border all barbarians is the Roman need to create a bogeyman, a possible threat justifying expenditures along the frontier (p. 518) and strengthening the powerful and ambitious leaders far from Rome against internal rivals (p. 524). These Romans needed to amplify the nature of the threat in simple friend-or-foe terms. Relationships on the ground were far more cordial and profitable than the literature suggests. What transpired, Halsall says, is neither an incursion nor a migration, but a slow-motion intermingling of various, unrelated peoples (2014, pp. 522 & 525). Each group seeped into the other. Halsall writes, "Frontier activity tended to be local, *ad hoc* and contingent" (p. 522; see generally, Goffart, 2006). Only the Romans gave these other tribes as a group a single label (barbarian, German), despite the fact that these little enclaves did not regard themselves as sharing a single culture with one another.[10] Nevertheless, scholars persist in using such comprehending labels to this day (p. 520).[11] For present purposes, we will concentrate on the relatively minor tribe that did eventually come to think of themselves as a unified people, i.e., the Franks.

Reflecting on the situation, it is remarkable how little there was of the Frankish people to commend them to have become so dominant that they secured nearly the entirety of France and held it more or less continuously into the modern era. Geary calls the Franks before Clovis "relatively insignificant and divided" (1988, p. 78). J.B. Bury (1967) writes that, instead of the Franks, "the Goths seemed almost certain to be the ultimate inheritors of all Gaul, and they had already acquired almost all Spain" (p. 214). What set the Franks apart in the early days,

---

10 In fact, writes Vedran Bileta (2016), Roman society started to refer to their own soldiers, of whatever ethnicity, as "barbarians" because they posed a threat to the social elite and also because they started to adopt certain practices from the border tribes, including names and battle tactics, out of pride in their acquired prowess (p. 35). Thus, use of the term "barbarian" was not straightforward.

Further complicating the nomenclature, Walter Goffart (2006) published an extensive plea to abandon the use of the terms "German" and "Germanic" when referring to tribes such as the Franks, because the term is an anachronism and inapt.

11 I would reply that although these tribes along the border may not have regarded themselves as a unit, for purposes of analysis we can do so, as long as we keep Halsall's words of caution in mind. Any description of a composite, which happens often in sociology for purposes of convenience, will tend to overlook variation within the group.

notes one expert, was superior leadership (Drinkwater, 2007, pp. 354–356).[12] In the literature, these leaders are sometimes designated as chiefs or chieftains; sometimes, as kings (Wallace-Hadrill, 1962, p. 70; see Canning, 1996, p. 16f). Geary resorts to using the German label *Heerkönig* (1988, p. 61). Initially, they were elected as military commanders and little more. Starting out, perhaps it would be most accurate to label Clovis a petty chieftain, though he would soon outgrow this nomenclature (Crisp, 2003, p. 37).

By tradition, the Franks in the era of Clovis assembled annually at *Warfeld* at a large open ground in order to deliberate about military objectives for the coming year and about leadership and its succession, inasmuch as Frankish "kings" were to be elected (de Bonnechose, 1856, p. 17; see Wood, 2013, quoting de Boulain-villiers, 1727; cf. Wood, 2022, p. 161).[13] This democratic practice created a sense of mutual accountability between the leader and the led. Furthermore, Salic Law, championed by Clovis, borrowed from the Frankish tradition a greater concern for the individual and his rights, unlike Roman law. The role of a king at that time was limited to issues of security and conquest. The king did not preside over the law, religion, or commerce in any meaningful sense.[14] Thus, he enjoyed only a limited authority (de Bonnechose, 1856, pp. 14 & 17; Gibbon, 1782/2020, ch. 38, part 1; contra Foucault, 1997, p. 25f). The king was a war leader, viewed by the Romans as something of a magistrate to keep their kinsmen in line (Wood, 2013, p. 109).[15] Gradually, under Clovis, and more rapidly under his heirs, these

---

12 For a complementary viewpoint, there are those who blame the collapse of the Roman Empire on *poor* leadership (see, e.g., Wood, 2013, p. 90; Foucault, 1997, p. 145). One author named Ferdinand Lot expresses doubts about these barbarian tribes as a "force for regeneration" for a stale and rigid regime, revitalizing the empire. Instead, Lot emphasizes their sheer brutality. Nevertheless, "Much depended on the quality of the individual leader" (Wood, 2013, p. 266). In each instance, the salient factor is leadership. A dissenting voice, to be fair, comes from Geary (1988) who ascribes the success of Clovis more to luck and the prior mixture of two comparable (and compatible) cultures than to his exertions (p. 89; but see p. 112). Certainly luck (or *fortuna*) does play a part in leadership generally, which does not necessarily nullify the importance of the leadership itself.

13 Because of this tradition, kings could not designate an heir (Bauer, 2010, p. 178; see Canning, 1996, p. 21). This need to choose a leader all over again each year jeopardized Frankish continuity – making the sustained success of the Merovingian dynasty all the more remarkable. Eastern empires tended to prefer that the heirs fight it out for supremacy, which had the benefit of keeping the realm intact, but which also had the detrimental effect of creating intrigue and oftentimes outright bloodshed in the imperial palace until a winner could emerge. Courtiers, mothers, and lovers often got in the act. Imperial succession in Rome was not too dissimilar. As Heather (2006) remarks, "Periodic conflict at the top was the price to be paid for the Empire's success in integrating elites across its vast domain" (p. 131). Such a process entailed violence, or what Heather calls "bouts of protracted instability that were inherent to the Roman political system" (2006, p. 391). He adds sardonically, "You don't hear of many retirements from the uppermost tiers of late Roman politics" (2006, p. 254). The alternative solution of primogeniture had not yet been instituted in Europe (Glassman, 2017, p. 1489).

14 Regarding commerce, see generally Sawyer (1977).

15 Ian Wood quotes Henri comte de Boulainvilliers, who in 1727 wrote *État de la France* (at vol. 1, p. 15): "Clovis was only the general of a free army, which had elected him to lead its undertakings, the

liberal features of Frankish life transmogrified into the hierarchical social structure known as feudalism that we commonly associate today with the Middle Ages (de Bonnechose, 1856, p. 17).[16] But that was to come many years later.

Here then is the situation facing a teenage war leader with Christian sympathies. Gaul as a geographic region had disintegrated politically into a variety of incompatible groupings, all aspiring to fill the resulting power vacuum. This region, sometimes referred to as transalpine Gaul (as opposed to cisalpine Gaul, held at the time by a king named Theodoric), cut westward from the northeast corner of the territory around the Massif Central, which is much further south along the Mediterranean coast. The Massif Central is located in the south-central region of Gaul – roughly the kingdom of the Burgundians. So, it is not exactly southeast of Franks, but due south. (See appendix.) Another tribe, the Alammani, were southeast of the Franks, and beyond them surrounded by the Mediterranean Sea were the Ostrogoths, in possession of present-day Italy.

Southwest of the Franks was the territory controlled by a Roman warlord holding territory between the British channel to the north and the Massif Central to the south. Beyond his territory on the left, further south and west and extending across the Pyrenees, were the Visigoths.[17] A smattering of other tribes filled the interstices.

Would-be usurpers and ambitious Roman generals competed for dominance throughout the empire, notwithstanding the infusion of barbarian peoples in the land (Wood, 2017, p. 17f). The Franks were only loosely affiliated among themselves! In addition, the Roman Catholic Church had come to influence the native peoples, the Galli, largely through the local authority of urban bishops; and even though the clergy as a class were not ostensibly political, they often governed local affairs (Wood, 2017, p. 85), as we shall see in a subsequent chapter. After all, a position in the church was one of the few outlets for the privileged and best educated young men, such that many of these bishops came from a Romanized aristocracy, an elite by any standard that was also familiar with the plight of the ordinary people throughout Gaul (Riddle, 2016, p. 81; see generally van Dam, 1985). That combination of Roman elite status with intimate contact with their people often proved to make these bishops formidable figures during the ensuing power struggles. Even so, the Christian faith was relatively new here, such that

---

glory and profit of which ought to have been common to all" (2013, p. 24). Elsewhere, Wood (1977) refers to the "double nature" of Frankish authority, as both the elected war leader of a tribe and as a provincial governor for Rome (p. 25). With time, Clovis collapsed these two authorities into one, as he would as well with divine sanction under the Roman Catholic Church.

16 In 2017, Susan Reynolds argued that the verbiage of "feudalism" is not altogether helpful when trying to understand the Middle Ages. Her effort to rethink the vocabulary by which scholars write about this era is notable, even though the term continues to be useful in many contexts.

17 The Visigoths had a much more extensive and enduring relationship with the Roman Empire. At one time, they controlled considerable territory. By 476 CE, writes Heather (2006), "Visigothic settlement had finally become a kingdom, stretching from the Loire in the north, to the Alps in the east, to the straits of Gibraltar in the south" (p. 417).

there were still many enclaves of pagan worship, while at the same time the other barbarian tribes tended to favor a heresy known as Arianism. Furthermore, on a global scale, the institutional church itself was increasingly split between the western/Roman Catholics and the eastern/Byzantine Orthodox (Wallace-Hadrill, 1962, p. 13).[18] Out of this complex web of circumstances arose a young leader who forever shaped the destiny of western Europe.

Any biography of the man Clovis will be impoverished.[19] The sheer passage of time, compounded by scant evidence and unreliable sources, has left us with a cartoon version of a ruthless barbarian miraculously favored in battle once he finally relents and is baptized. Yet he then presides over the bloody and superstitious descent into what are known as the Dark Ages (Daly, 1994, p. 620).[20] The truth about Clovis is otherwise.

We do know that, according to William Daly (1994), upon his ascension in 481 CE, Clovis had inherited a "pro-imperial and anti-Visigoth orientation" from his father. Furthermore, we do have evidence that, at an early age, he considered adopting Arianism (a religion quite common among the barbarian tribes, a religion which had been judged in 325 CE to be heretical); yet he was sufficiently acquainted with Roman Catholicism that he knew at least the rudiments of its doctrine (Daly, 1994, p. 633). He was also always quite deferential to the church and its clergy (Daly, 1994, p. 641; Bury, 1967, p. 214), as well as being kindly disposed to its saints. Sometime during his reign, he was formally received into the church and baptized; legend has it that it had been urged upon him by his wife for quite a long time, but precipitated at last during a crucial battle on Christmas Day (Daly, 1994, p. 637). The actual year of his conversion is a matter of some dispute (Shanzer, 2012, p. xiii; see generally Pestano, 2015–16).

The forms of Roman authority could no longer hold the region of Gaul together. Clovis saw an opportunity to collaborate with the church in order to

---

18 So also the Roman Empire itself, as a practical necessity (see, e.g., Heather, 2006, pp. 29f & 130).

19 Jan-Benedict Steenkamp (2020) has offered a succinct and useful mini-biography for students of leadership.

20 Foucault (1997) recounts some of the epithets for the Frankish barbarian, such as unpolished, rough, haughty, faithless, restless, cruel, fickle, and fierce (p. 149). Nevertheless, he is careful to note that, in point of fact, "The barbarian is the opposite of the savage" (p. 195).

   Arguably the most eminent contemporary source about Clovis was Gregory of Tours, who died in 594 CE. His *Historiae* (1974) has influenced scholars through the ages, despite numerous doubts about the veracity of his version of events (see, e.g., Naidos, 2015; Wood, 1994, pp. 2 & 32; Hen, 1993; van Dam, 1985, section IV; Wood, 1985). Wallace-Hadrill (1962) writes that Gregory "makes . . . some severe demands on the intelligence of the historian" (p. 69). Pestano (2015–16) blames many of the more obvious errors in Gregory's account to subsequent interpolators who had their own agenda. Wallace-Hadrill goes on to speculate that the successor dynasty (the Carolingians) had little reason to create or preserve the historical record of the Merovingians. If anything, after the acclaim afforded to Clovis, the stature of subsequent chieftains in his bloodline declined, such that the Carolingians deserved to govern in their stead (p. 91). The historical record available to us today suffers as a consequence.

unify Gaul, which gave him the tactical advantage of cloaking territorial disputes as religious wars (Bauer, 2010, p. 173; Steenkamp, 2020, p. 26), even though it appears that religion was rarely a genuine motive (Wood, 2017, p. 51). One might say that, under Clovis, Christianity helped to unify Gaul, and Clovis helped to unify church and state (Riddle, 2016, p. 82).[21]

It is worth noting that Clovis had married Clotilda, daughter of a king from nearby Burgundians with whom he entered into a pact (Henault, 1762, p. 2; see Crisp, 2003).[22] As it happens, Clotilda was the only royal daughter in the vicinity who was also a Roman Catholic. Later, she would be canonized by the church (de Bonnechose, 1856, p. 12). In fact, one of the Franks' earliest victories under Clovis came against these very Burgundians – kinsmen of his wife – after they (the Burgundian royal family) murdered Clotilda's father in order to win the throne. Seen in this light, Clovis was only upholding his wife's family's honor during an intramural struggle.[23]

At the time Clovis was elected king, at the tender age of 15, the Franks occupied a small portion of Gaul. His father had been a relatively minor chieftain (see Wood, 2013, p. 31). Making matters worse, his father had left him a small fighting force, although the exact numbers are in dispute (Laing, 2000, p. 86; Gibbon, 1782/2020, ch. 38, part 1). It could have been as few as 400 to 500.[24] To the

---

21 Wallace-Hadrill (1962) explains that western Christianity emerged from the influence of Augustine, which repudiated the idea of a state religion or the ambition to create heaven-on-earth (p. 15; contra Heather, 2006, p. 233–235). For this reason, bishops were less interested in Christendom as a political project and more interested in Christianity as a faith (p. 16). The church saw itself not as a rival institution to the royal household, but as a parallel or complementary institution (p. 15). Clovis would find that posture congenial. By the same token, the church repudiated the old Roman belief in emperor-worship, so that no church had to subordinate itself to the prevailing civic authorities. For these reasons, Augustine urged leaders of every stripe to exercise humility (see, e.g., Ray, 2020, ch. 3).

Because of the collapse of a unifying Roman hierarchy centered in Rome (which at the time was occupied by barbarian heretics), regional bishops in Gaul enjoyed considerably more autonomy (see Wood, 2022, p. 20, citing Brown, *The Rise of Western Christendom*). They also tended to compete with one another for prestige. Also, one sees the emergence of monasteries, oftentimes sponsored by local families, with considerable independence of their own. For these reasons, the "church" in that era was only loosely unified (Wallace-Hadrill, 1962, p. 18; Geary, 1988, p. 229). In point of fact, it was undergoing a transition into the powerful institution it was to become later (Wood, 2017).

22 Clotilda was not only a royal princess, of higher rank than Clovis at the time of their marriage, but she was also the sole heiress of a king's treasure. She was reputed to be elegant and wise, a delight to Clovis. It may have served his purpose as well that she was the lone eligible Catholic princess in the region (Crisp, 2003, pp. 59–71).

23 The story is more convoluted (see Gibbon, 1782/2020; Crisp, 2003, p. 71).

24 Roger Collins (1999) has explained that soldiers at the time were not always committed to ethnic alliances. They freely joined one army or another based on a variety of factors, such as which commander appeared to be more likely to gain them booty. During his reign, Clovis commanded many non-Franks, and many Franks fought for rival leaders (p. 113; see Ward-Perkins, 2005, p. 50f). Thus, as he consolidated his power, Clovis attracted more and more fighting men to his

east, the kinsmen of Clovis held no fear of him and his people, inasmuch as they were probably preoccupied fending off the Hun (Drinkwater, 2007, p. 362f; cf. Goffart, 2006). Nearby warlords tried to retain power in the hands of the remaining Romans (Bauer, 2010, p. 172; Wood, 2017, p. 17).[25] The Burgundians were amassed to his south; the Visigoths, on his southwest (see map). A number of lesser barbarian tribes were also scattered about.

To the far south, Theodoric the Ostrogoth held what is known today as Italy. From there, Theodoric practiced wide-ranging diplomacy with other barbarian tribes, including the Vandals, Visigoths, and Burgundians. Nevertheless, Theodoric actually married the sister of Clovis and thereby concluded a pact with the Franks in 500 CE (Henault, 1762, p. 3; cf. Crisp, 2003, 54). Theodoric's real quarrel, truth be told, was with the newly created Byzantine Empire headquartered far away in Constantinople, for the Christians there wanted the city of Rome and its environs back under their control. Theodoric brokered peace in the north because he did not need other headaches on his border.[26]

From his side of the Alps, then, Theodoric the Great presumed to mentor the various tribal leaders to the north, hoping to help them keep the peace and – not incidentally – stay out of his territory. He did not want them up there clashing with one another and drawing him into their internecine disputes. Among these tribes, the most prominent rival to Clovis in Gaul was Alaric II, king of the Visigoths. Alaric and Theodoric (and the rest of the barbarian tribes) were Arians and not Roman Catholic, so in this specific regard the Franks were unusual. Also,

---

standard, which is how he converted a small fighting force loyal to his father into an overpowering army. In this fashion, his reign exemplifies the adage that success breeds success (see also Wood, 2013, p. 290; Geary, 1988, p. 88). For example, as Clovis defeated nearby armies and won more and more territory, the standoffish Ripuarian Franks who had stayed beyond the borderlands on the proverbial sidelines now drifted into Gaul opportunistically and put themselves under the command of Clovis (Wallace-Hadrill, 1962, p. 73). Wood (1994) refers to these armies as "heterogeneous warbands" (p. 39; see also Geary, 1988, p. 56). Halsall refers to "the leader and his retinue (*Gefolgschaft*)" (2014, p. 517; see generally Mathisen, 2019). The significant detail that should not be overlooked is that individual warriors in such a system could choose whom to follow (Heather, 2006, p. 453).

25 In fact, Clovis campaigned first against a Roman warlord nearby whose father had once exiled his own father Childeric. Being relatively shorthanded, Clovis was accompanied on this campaign by another petty chieftain named Chararic, who at the decisive battle held back until it became obvious that Clovis would win. Only then did he join the fray. Clovis won the defeated warriors to his side and then, in retribution for Chararic's hesitation, turned against him. The warriors of Chararic, ashamed of their chief's perfidy, readily abandoned him for Clovis, thereby increasing the fighting force dedicated to Clovis that much more (Crisp, 2003, pp. 40–43). In this way, Clovis augmented his military power while dismantling rivals.

26 Because they had had their hands full nearby, the Byzantines had deputized Theodoric previously to retake the peninsula from the Hun. They expected him to govern in their stead. Over time, however, the Christian emperor decided from a distance that it was unseemly for the land of Rome to be governed by heretics, which is why a Christian war leader such as Clovis in the vicinity caught the emperor's diplomatic attention (Wallace-Hadrill, 1962, pp. 33–36).

Clovis demonstrated familiarity with Roman forms of administration, thereby improving the reach and efficiency of his power, making him a more competent executive (Daly, 1994, p. 646). All the same, Theodoric the Great viewed the young leader to the north as an impressionable ward.

Once, for example, when Clovis had been wronged by a specific chieftain of a lesser tribe, he pursued this leader and then chased his people into lands controlled by Theodoric. Such was Theodoric's standing that he wrote to Clovis, conceding that the young king had been wronged and was within his rights to execute the perfidious chief, but that now it would be unseemly to cross the border in order to wreak further havoc. It is also likely that Theodoric did not need the incursion, which he would have been expected to repel. Furthermore, it was known that when he conquered a people, Clovis tended to want to eradicate entire bloodlines, whereas Theodoric was probably more cosmopolitan and so favored keeping the elite families across the various tribes intact (Drinkwater, 2007, p. 346; Crisp, 2003; see also Wood, 1994, p. 42). Whether he meant what he said or not, Theodoric tried to persuade his neighbors to the north that a network of intermarriage among the royal households would contribute to regional peace (Crisp, 2003, pp. 1–20). Clovis had married a Burgundian, as we saw; Theodoric had married a Frankish relative of Clovis; and Alaric II had married an Ostrogoth relative of Theodoric (Crisp, 2003). As it happens, Theodoric persuaded his youthful brother-in-law to stand down and accept the status quo. Clovis relented.[27]

Nevertheless, Theodoric was at the same time warning other chieftains in Europe that Clovis was demonstrating two things worth noting: ambitions to expand and real skill at conducting war (Daly, 1994, p. 643). And now he was poised close to Theodoric's northern border. During the resulting lull in tensions, after Theodoric persuaded Clovis to stand down, Clovis expanded in other directions, so that soon he controlled land from the Rhine and the Rhone rivers north and westward to the sea (Drinkwater, 2007, p. 345; de Bonnechose, 1856, p. 14). That still left a considerable chunk of Gaul to the south in the hands of Burgundians (to the south) and Visigoths (to the southwest).

With the Burgundians ensconced in the rugged highlands and formally subordinated to him, Clovis next turned his attention against Alaric II to the southwest. Theodoric ostensibly hoped to broker a peace, while secretly pledging to side

---

27 Toward the end of his reign, Clovis reverted to the practice of wiping out rival bloodlines, including his own relatives! Wood (1994) notes that his practice of consolidating power by turning against his kinfolk would continue after his death and help to explain the decades of civil war that routinely engulfed the Merovingian dynasty, as blood relatives plotted and battled one another for supremacy – all without seriously jeopardizing the integrity of the nation (p. 101). As Wood puts it, "The Merovingians were regularly at each other's throats" (p. 89). The implication is that if Clovis had not eliminated his kinfolk, they would have eliminated him (Crisp, 2003, p. 44). So, we might say that, just as Frankish warriors did not fight along ethnic lines but proved to be opportunists, blood relations in the royal family did not make for natural political allies with one another.

with Alaric against the long-haired Franks if it came to open warfare (Bachrach, 2012, p. 24). The problem was that the Catholic emperor in Constantinople had launched an invasion along the coast of the Apennine Peninsula, hoping to retake Rome, a tactic requiring Theodoric to devote his forces to thwarting this assault (Daly, 1994, p. 644). Consequently, he had nothing left to give to Alaric when the conflict with Clovis began. It turns out that Anastasius, the reigning (Christian) emperor, saw in Clovis a viable ally and coreligionist conveniently poised on his adversary's doorstep (Shanzer, 2012, p. xii). It is unclear whether Anastasius had urged Clovis to attack Alaric at the same time that the emperor's ships were landing in Theodoric's backyard, but it certainly looked suspicious inasmuch as he had deployed envoys to the court of Clovis more than once before the date of the decisive battle between Clovis and Alaric at Vouillé (Bachrach, 2012, p. 22; see Mathisen, 2022, p. 415f; Geary, 1988, p. 87). It is unclear what the various bishops in the territory controlled by Alaric did behind the scenes to aid and assist the cause of their marauding coreligionist from Paris, although the experts disagree with one another on the level of their involvement (Bachrach, 2012, p. 23; Gibbon, 1782/2020, ch. 38, part 2; contra Naidos, 2014, p. 45; Wood, 1994, p. 47). At the very least, the conversion of Clovis threatened "the internal stability of his neighbors" (Geary, 1988, p. 86). Peter Brown claims that the Arian barbarians were a tight-knit warrior class precisely because they were so widely despised (or ignored) by the Catholic underclass; they had to stick together out of self-defense. He then writes, "The Franks were the exception that proved the rule" (1971, p. 125).

Alaric II had an additional disadvantage going into this war. Not only was his sponsor Theodoric preoccupied with repulsing the onslaught on his own shores, and the church was opposed to his heretical faith, but also Alaric's finances at the time were paltry, and many of his best fighting men had gone to settle in the Iberian Peninsula as farmers (James, 1982, p. 18).[28] In light of these circumstances, Clovis had an unimpeded chance to defeat his foe. With superior horses and Roman tactics – and the simultaneous attack on Alaric by the Burgundians – the Franks swept southward.

Finding himself on the wrong side of a river with no bridges in sight, and seeing the enemy encamped on the banks barely a stone's throw away, Clovis was led in the night by local villagers to a secret ford upstream, which gained him the element of surprise. Waking to find the Franks on the near side of the water – somehow – the Visigoths reportedly fled in confusion (Gibbon, 1782/2020, ch.

---

28 The Visigoths had been migrating westward across Europe in search of someplace that could feed them, and although southern France was attractive for several reasons, they had to stop somewhere to grow crops (Wallace-Hadrill, 1962, p. 23ff). For a more detailed account of their peculiar saga, see Geary, 1988, pp. 69–71. The Iberian Peninsula, guarded more or less by a mountain range, met these requirements; so, in many ways, the Visigoths were not motivated to abandon their Spanish farms in order to hold Aquitaine by force.

38, part 2). It is rumored that at the fateful battle of Vouillé in 507 CE Clovis him-self killed Alaric (Henault, 1762, p. 3). Under the Franks' unrelenting pressure, and now without their leader, the Visigoths had nowhere to go but west across the Pyrenees, to their families, farms, and safety (Shanzer, 2012, p. ix). Clovis had won the field.

Because of his victory, Clovis controlled much of what is now France (Wood, 1994, p. 57). Clearly, from that moment, Theodoric regarded Clovis less as a vas-sal or protégé and more as a formidable adversary.[29] And rightfully so. At the same time, Anastasius in Constantinople shifted considerable status onto his victorious ally (Esders, 2022, p. 348; Mathisen, 2012a, p. 87). Clovis accepted his Byzantine honors as a validation of his rule as a kind of latter-day Roman emperor, which was surely not the original intent of Anastasius, who thought of *himself* as the sole imperial successor (Bauer, 2010, p. 175; see generally Mathisen, 2012b). But the interpretation that Clovis put on being named consul was relatively harm-less, as these things go. At least the indigenous people of Gaul and their Roman landowners were purportedly impressed by the honorific (Wallace-Hadrill, 1962, p. 75; see Foucault, 1997, p. 72).[30]

It does appear that Clovis finally had no reason to expand further. He turned Paris into the capital, championed a new legal code throughout the regime blending Frankish custom with Roman principles (Neumann, n.d.; Daly, 1994, pp. 647–655; Wood, 1994, ch. 7; Gibbon, 1782/2020, ch. 38, part 2),[31] and con-voked the various bishops to the First Council of Orléans in 511 CE in order to discuss their interrelationships throughout the realm going forward under a single monarch (Daly, 1994, pp. 655–662).[32] For instance, Clovis agreed that church property was not to be treated as booty (Riddle, 2016, p. 82). From that day forward, one can speak of a cohesive Frankish church (Shanzer, 2012, p. xxi).[33] When it came to the law and religion, therefore, it was Clovis who gathered the experts, set the agenda, and reserved the privilege of approving what they would devise (Daly, 1994, p. 656; see also Riddle, 2016, p. 82). That is to say, he expected the regime to become at least somewhat uniform throughout the realm.

---

29 In fact, upon the retreat of the Visigoths, which he was powerless to prevent, Theodoric at last hastened to recover what he could in southwestern Gaul, ensuring that Clovis never reached the Mediterranean Sea (Bauer, 2010, p. 175). This was apparently all Theodoric could salvage.

30 Ian Wood (2017) cites evidence that the barbarian leaders did not set out to displace the Roman Empire so much as wrest control and restore its grandeur (pp. 21 & 27). They had little interest in its "collapse."

31 Canning differentiates popular custom as law from the royal code and from royal decrees (1996, p. 24).

32 Bryan Ward-Perkins (2005) writes that Alaric had done much the same thing on behalf of the Visigoths in the sixth century (p. 76).

33 James Haun (2013) remarks that the resulting structure was not a monolith. In fact, the bishops more or less agreed to a kind of federation of bishoprics in which each bishop enjoyed consider-able discretion to run things according to local custom, as long as they yielded to the overarching will of the king (p. 32; see also p. 40). It was Charlemagne many generations later who insisted on a more uniform system.

Toward the end, Clovis was engaged in presiding over his domain, now known as *Francia*, but he did so without being dictatorial. He was cognizant of the issues, sensitive to balancing everybody's rights, and especially tender to the plight of the poor, the widow, and the orphan. He was not especially cruel or violent, out of proportion to his purpose and his time, yet he did consider it prudent to kill other chieftains routinely, including his own relatives (Innes, 2004, p. 170).[34] Commentators opine that, on the whole, it was less destructive to assassinate a few pretenders in the dark of night than fight full-scale battles for supremacy. Historians accept that Clovis consolidated his power by killing any rivals from among his own kin (Wood, 1977, p. 10). By the same token, from the scant evidence that survives, Clovis honored the saints in his midst, appreciated fine music, and built a famous basilica (Daly, 1994, p. 662). That basilica, known as The Church of the Holy Apostles, affirmed the Nicene Creed against heresy and served as his royal mausoleum (Pessoa, 2019, p. 262f). The bishops he had convened at Orléans testified to his concern for the faith (Wood, 2022, p. 150, quoting from the *epistola ad regem*). As Daly puts it, the record about Clovis "discloses a Romanized German king, foresighted, knowledgeable, diligent, innovative, securely in control of his problems, and attentive to providing equity for all his subjects" (1994, p. 663).

In contradistinction to the image of a wild-haired, brutal, and superstitious harbinger of the Dark Ages, cloaked in the rough tunics of havoc, Clovis actually established a hybrid regime with surprising sophistication – a nation that persisted more or less intact until the Revolution in 1789, more than a thousand years later. Historians sometimes refer to France as a "successor state" to post-imperial Rome (Ando, 2008, p. 35). There is little reason to blame him for the resulting descent into the Dark Ages. The redoubtable Gibbon puts it this way: "The Franks, or French, are the only people of Europe who can deduce a perpetual succession from the conquerors of the Western empire. But their conquest of Gaul was followed by ten centuries of anarchy and ignorance" (1782/2020, ch. 38, part 2). By the era of Charlemagne, with the benefit of hindsight, historians attributed the decline *after* Clovis to inferior leadership – a state of affairs that the new Carolingian dynasty felt obliged to infuse with renewed vigor, in order to

---

34 Wallace-Hadrill (1962) notes that "no sense of moral obloquy or incongruity pursued them when they left the shrines to cut the throats of unloved kinsmen" (p. 78). Clovis and his heirs were men of blood for whom "fighting was as much the business of good, as carousing was of foul weather" (p. 77). Steenkamp (2020) puts it succinctly: "His crude, cunning, and savage qualities are painfully evident" (p. 22). Bishop Gregory excused this savagery, as long as the Franks served as the scourge of God. These barbarians were admittedly flawed instruments of divine will (p. 69). He called Clovis *magnus et pugnator egregius* – that is, "a great and magnificent fighter" (1962, p. 72). He tolerated the contradiction of such a murderous Christian. Wood (2017) reminds his reader thus: "The brutality and destruction, however, were geographically confined and chronologically short-lived" (p. 22). Besides, he added elsewhere, "however much of a royal virtue it might be, piety alone was not enough" (p. 68).

keep the Frankish state intact.[35] Once again, the differentiator was thought to be leadership.

In the year 511 CE, Clovis died at the age of 45 after a consequential reign of 30 years (Henault, 1762, p. 5).[36] It was his name that was later modernized as Louis (James, 1982, p. 26; Gibbon, 1782/2020, chapter 38, part I). And, of course, in our own day, the name of the nation itself derives from that scattered, opportunistic confederacy of tribes unified under Clovis known as the Franks.[37]

References

Ando, C. (2008, Spring). "Decline, fall, and transformation." *Journal of Late Antiquity. 1*(1): 31–60.

Bachrach, B. (2012). "Vouillé & the decisive battle phenomenon in late antique Gaul." In Mathisen, R. & Shanzer, D. (eds.). *The battle of Vouillé, 507 CE: Where France began* (pp. 11–42). De Gruyter.

Bauer, S.W. (2010). *The history of the Medieval world: From the conversion of Constantine to the first Crusades.* W. W. Norton & Co.

Bileta, V. (2016). "The last legions: The 'barbarization' of military identity in the Late Roman West." *Tabula: časopis Filozofskog fakulteta, Sveučilište Jurja Dobrile u Puli.* (14): 22–42.

Brown, P. (1971). *The world of Late Antiquity, AD 150–750.* Thames & Hudson, Ltd.

Bury, J.B. (1967). *The invasion of Europe by the Barbarians.* W. W. Norton & Co.

Canning, J. (1996). *A history of medieval political thought, 300–1450.* Routledge.

Collins, R. (1999). *Early Medieval Europe, 300–1000* (2nd ed.). St. Martins Press.

Crisp, R. (2003). "Marriage and alliance in the Merovingian kingdoms, 481–639." (Doctoral dissertation. Ohio State University).

Daly, W. (1994, July). "Clovis: How barbaric, how pagan?" *Speculum. 69*(3): 619–664.

de Bonnechose, E. (1856). *History of France: From the invasion of the Franks under Clovis, to the accession of Louis Philippe* (2nd ed., W. Robson, trans.). Routledge.

Drinkwater, J. (2007). *The Alamanni and Rome, 213–496: Caracalla to Clovis* (ch. 9). Oxford University Press.

Esders, S. (2022). "The Merovingians and Byzantium: Diplomatic, military, and religious issues, 500–700." In Effros, B. & Moreira, I. (eds.). *The Oxford handbook of the Merovingian world* (ch. 16). Oxford University Press.

Foucault, M. (1997). *"Society must be defended": Lectures at the College de France, 1975–76* (D. Macey, trans.). Picador.

Geary, P. (1988). *Before France and Germany: The creation and transformation of the Merovingian world.* Oxford University Press.

---

35 Janet Nelson (2020) questions whether the term "state" would fit the civic order at the time of Clovis. She considers an alternative nomenclature (e.g., p. 35).

36 Collins (1999) cites the *Liber Pontificalis* (i.e., the official papal biographies) as evidence that Clovis was still alive and paying tribute in the year 513 (p. 114). Regarding the actual dates in the biography of Clovis, see generally Pestano, 2015–16.

37 Potter (2021) writes, "States that expand very rapidly are often very unstable" (p. 74, citing Alexander the Great and Genghis Kahn). Attila the Hun is another vivid example of this. Yet the regime established by Clovis endured, despite instabilities, which makes his leadership all the more noteworthy.

Gibbon, E. (1782/2020). *History of the decline and fall of the Roman empire* (vol. III, ch. 38). Project Gutenberg. Retrieved 24 July 2020 from www.gutenberg.org/files/25717/25717-h/25717-h.htm#Clink382HCH0001.

Glassman, R. (2017). *The origins of democracy in tribes, city-states, and nation-states* (vol. I). Springer.

Goffart, W. (2006). *Barbarian tides: The migration age and the late Roman Empire.* University of Pennsylvania Press.

Graceffa, A. (2022). "Writing the history of Merovingian Gaul." In Effros, B. & Moreira, I. (eds.). *The Oxford handbook of the Merovingian world* (ch. 3). Oxford University Press.

Halsall, G. (2014). "Two worlds become one: A 'counter-intuitive' view of the Roman Empire and 'Germanic' migration." *German History. 32*(4): 515–532.

Haun, J. (2013, May). "A new system of power: The Franks and the Catholic church in post-Roman Gaul." (Doctoral dissertation. University of Texas at Arlington).

Heather, P. (2006). *The fall of the Roman Empire: A new history of Rome and the Barbarians.* Oxford University Press.

Hen, Y. (1993). "Clovis, Gregory of Tours, and pro-Merovingian propaganda." *Revue belge de Philologie et d'Histoire. 71*(2): 271–276.

Henault, M. (1762). *A new chronological abridgement of the history of France, containing the publick transactions of that kingdom, from Clovis to Lewis XI: Their wars, battles, sieges &c, their laws, manners, customs, &c.* (Mr. Nugent, trans.). J. Nourse, opposite Katherine-Street in the Strand, Bookseller in Ordinary to His Majesty.

Innes, M. (2004). *State and society in the early Middle Ages: The middle Rhine valley, 400–1000.* Cambridge University Press.

James, E. (1982). *The origins of France: From Clovis to the Capetians, 500–1000.* St. Martin's Press.

Laing, J. (2000). *Warriors of the dark ages* (ch. 5). Sutton Publishing.

Mathisen, R.W. (2022). "Alors commença la France." In Effros, B. & Moreira, I. (eds.). *The Oxford handbook of the Merovingian world* (ch. 19). Oxford University Press.

Mathisen, R.W. (2019). "The end of the western Roman Empire in the fifth century CE: Barbarian auxiliaries, independent military contractors, and civil wars." In Drijvers, J. & Lenski, N. (eds.). *The fifth century: Age of transformation* (pp. 137–156) [Proceedings of the 12th Biennial Shifting Frontiers in Late Antiquity conference]. Edipuglia.

Mathisen, R.W. (2012a). "Vouillé, Voulon, and the location of the campus Vogladensis." In Mathisen, R. & Shanzer, D. (eds.). *The battle of Vouillé, 507 CE: Where France began* (pp. 43–62). De Gruyter.

Mathisen, R.W. (2012b). "Clovis, Anastasius, and political status in 508 CE: The Frankish aftermath of the Battle of Vouillé." In Mathisen, R. & Shanzer, D. (eds.). *The battle of Vouillé, 507 CE: Where France began* (pp. 79–110). De Gruyter.

Naidos, M. (2015). "Perceptions of the past in Merovingian historiography: The case of Gregory of Tours' Historia Francorum." *Revista electrônica sobre Antiguidade e Medievo. 4*(2): 70–89.

Naidos, M. (2014). "The Gallo-Roman bishops, the legitimacy of the Merovingian dynasty and the Christianization of Merovingian kingship." *Revista electrônica sobre Antiguidade e Medievo. 3*(2): 40–58.

Neumann, J. (n.d.). "The laws of Clovis in the *Lex Salica* and the transition from Gaul to Francia." Retrieved 18 July 2020 from www.academia.edu/10395717/The_laws_of_Clovis_in_the_Lex_Salica_and_the_transition_from_Gaul_to_Francia.

Pessoa, T. (2019). "The making of Merovingian Paris: The Christianization of a Gallo-Roman city." *Nuntius Antiquus. 15*(1): 249–278.

Pestano, D. (2015–6). "Clovis, king of the Franks: Towards a new chronology (9 parts)." *Dark Age History*. Retrieved 16 September 2020 from https://darkagehistory.blogspot. com/2015/06/clovisking-of-frankstowards-new_9.html.

Potter, D. (2021). *Disruption: Why things change*. Oxford University Press.

Pufendorf, S. (1695/2013). *An introduction to the history of the principal kingdoms and states of Europe* (J. Crull, trans.). Liberty Fund.

Ray, C. (2020). *Defining statesmanship: A comparative political theory analysis*. Lexington Books.

Reimitz, H. (2019). "*Pax inter utramque gentum*: The Merovingians, Byzantium and the history of Frankish identity." In Esders, S., Fox, Y., Hen, Y. & Sarti, L. (eds.). *East and West in the early Middle Ages: The Merovingian kingdoms in Mediterranean perspective* (ch. 3). Cambridge University Press.

Reynolds, S. (2017). *The Middle Ages without Feudalism: Essays in criticism and comparison on the Medieval West*. Routledge.

Riddle, J. (2016). *A history of the Middle Ages, 300–1500* (2nd ed.). Rowman & Littlefield.

Ruckert, J.M.M. (2011). "Romans and Goths in late antique Gaul: Aspects of political and cultural assimilation in the Fifth Century AD." (Masters thesis. Durham University). Retrieved Durham E-Theses from http://etheses.dur.ac.uk/708/.

Sawyer, P.H. (1977). "Kings and merchants." In Sawyer, P.H. & Wood, I. (eds.). *Early Medieval kingship* (ch. 6). School of History, University of Leeds.

Shanzer, D. (2012). "Foreword." In Mathisen, R. & Shanzer, D. (eds.). *The battle of Vouillé, 507 CE: Where France began*. De Gruyter.

Steenkamp, J.-B. (2020). *Time to lead: Lessons for today's leaders from bold decisions that changed history*. Fast Company.

van Dam, R. (1985). *Leadership and community in late antique Gaul*. University of California Press.

Wallace-Hadrill, J.M. (1962). *The barbarian west, AD 400–1000: The Early Middle Ages*. Harper Torchbook.

Ward-Perkins, B. (2005). *The fall of Rome and the end of civilization*. Oxford University Press.

Wood, I. (2022). *The Christian economy in the early Medieval West: Towards a temple society*. Punctum Books.

Wood, I. (2017). *The transformation of the Roman west*. Arc Humanities Press.

Wood, I. (2013). *The modern origins of the early Middle Ages*. Oxford University Press.

Wood, I. (1994). *The Merovingian kingdoms, 450–751*. Longman.

Wood, I. (1985). "Gregory of Tours and Clovis." *Revue belge de Philologie et d'Histoire. 63*(2): 249–272.

Wood, I. (1977). "Kings, kingdoms and consent." In Sawyer, P.H. & Wood, I. (eds.). *Early Medieval kingship* (ch. 1). School of History, University of Leeds.

2

THE CHARISMA OF CLOVIS

A standard analysis of the leadership of an ancient chieftain might focus on his charisma, properly citing the work of Max Weber (1947). Weber notes the divine origin of the leader's authority (p. 359), which Clovis could claim on three fronts: Frankish, Catholic, and Roman. First, he was purportedly the direct descendant of a pagan god. Second, unlike his rivals throughout Europe, he was baptized into the Roman Catholic Church, having shown a pattern of deference to the saints and bishops since before his ascension. He had married a devout princess, who later became a saint in her own right. He conspired with the Christian emperor in Constantinople to help him take back Rome. Clovis authorized the building of a place of worship in Paris. It's reported that it was only because of his conversion that he won an unlikely victory in battle. Lest we forget, his career began with the execution of a warrior who had objected to his policy of returning sacred objects rather than apportion them as booty. More than one commentator had reason to allege that Clovis was carrying out the mission of the church in subduing the pagans and the heretics, helping the church in Francia to establish its authority, even if his methods were cruel and vainglorious. Third, to the extent that Clovis was regarded by the locals as the latest in a long line of emperors, we might recall that the Roman emperor had been established as *"pontifex maximus,* supreme priest, of all public religions" (Haun, 2013, p. 15). Whether by virtue of his pagan ancestry, his Christian faith, or his occupying the role of Roman emperor, Clovis could certainly claim divine sanction for his leadership. According to early medieval political thought, the king was to be treated as both a powerful man and an embodiment of God's will (Haun, 2013, p. 20, citing Kantorowicz, 1957).

Furthermore, since charisma does not inhere in the person, like a trait or characteristic, but instead is a product of the perception of others, Weber notes the element of a follower's enthusiasm (p. 359), which for Clovis can be said to have

DOI: 10.4324/9781003297802-2

"snowballed" as he picked up fresh armies during his campaigns. They switched their allegiance to him, in part because he proved to be successful on the battlefield. The fact that he continued to conquer others only validated their loyalty (Weber, 1947, p. 360). The bishops also became increasingly enthused about their Christian king (Haun, 2013). Bishop Avitus of Vienne, for example, wrote to the new king, celebrating his coronation. "Divine Providence," he wrote, "has found the arbiter of our age" (quoted in Haun, 2013, p. 30).

The anthropologist Clifford Geertz writes about the topic of charisma and what he calls the symbolics of power. For purposes of illustration, he describes three historical figures, one of whom was Mulay Hassan I, king of Morocco, whose reign in the nineteenth century exemplifies charisma as an attribution by followers regarding a vigorous and willful leader. Geertz asserts that the numinous character of a leader could be based on the fact that what a leader accomplishes proves that he has the blessing of Allah. In other words, success validates his authority. In this way, Hasan resembles a younger Clovis.

Geertz (1977) explains that, according to Moroccan culture, Allah rewards forceful men. Accordingly, politics then was, in his words, a never-ending clash of personalities. The clashing was not disruptive of civic order; it was constitutive. This is an important point. If you cannot fight for yourself, then you have no business ruling others. He writes that "one genuinely possesses only what one can defend" (p. 162). And the one who most thoroughly imposes his will deserves to rule. Geertz calls this a warrior monarchy, which is largely what Clovis represents as well. The one who possesses this supreme power can govern as he likes, without accounting to other men, because he has been endowed by Allah to do as he pleases. But then, as a practical matter, if he wants to continue to do so across time, he will be required to suppress (or at least discourage) challenges to his supremacy repeatedly, challenges from within and from without.

Charisma in that Moroccan culture was associated with movement, vigor, almost a restlessness, as though energy itself were the sacred gift.[1] Not for Hasan the sedentary life of a royal court, as though he were the center of the cosmos radiating order outward; instead, he must be seen to sweep across the realm, always doing something (p. 162). And, as Geertz adds, he must move about in an unpredictable manner, spontaneously, leaving his subjects insecure, wondering

---

1 Until the Merovingian dynasty ended with a coup in 751 CE, charisma among the Franks had been symbolized in part by one's long hair (Goosman, 2012). Originally, long hair symbolized virility, but then also social status, becoming (in his words) "a *conditio sine qua non* for Frankish kingship" (p. 246). A boy's hair was protected by law and cared for with unguents and elaborate combing (p. 240). The loss of that hair brought shame and disqualified a man from serving in a leadership position until it grew back. Goosman even finds evidence that it was considered better to be killed outright than to be shorn (p. 242). When Clovis "Christianized" the Franks, some of these pagan traditions became co-opted, so that the long hair of the warrior class was now associated with the prodigious strength of the Old Testament judge Samson. It thereby continued to signify charisma, or at least a necessary condition for leadership.

where he might show up next. That is, the king must make his presence known and move on, so that the center of authority could visit anywhere, inasmuch as the "center" was the person of the king and not a capital city or palace (p. 163). Ultimately, the king must live an unsettled life, waging a tireless campaign of dominating lesser men. Hasan ended his days on a strenuous and misguided tour that left him depleted and weak. He was the last such king to govern Morocco. Geertz writes, "Immobilized, Moroccan kings were as dead as Hasan, their [charisma] impotent and theoretical" (p. 167).[2]

The youthful Clovis, who executed a subordinate on the review field with his battle-ax simply because he could, embodies this image of the warrior king who exerts his power as he pleases, strategically and thoroughly by means of violence. Clovis possessed this kind of charisma, and he saw to the extermination of rivals, by fair means or foul. This capacity for ruthlessness attracted warriors to his banner.

The interesting thing is that eventually, having command of the region – a region far beyond his youthful imagining – Clovis stopped campaigning. He established a capital city, gathered experts to unify the land (both its law and its religion), and contented himself to preside – not ending his days in perpetual conflict, looking for dragons to slay, and not making an exhibition of himself like Hasan. It appears that Clovis, having secured his place by means of intrigue and violence, matured into a stable and benign presence, without thereby losing status.[3] He transitioned from relying on relationships of domination, relentlessly questing against others, to competent administration, governing inward (Foucault, 1997, p. 223). He graduated from participating in a continent-wide grid of opposing forces to a project of consolidating Francia (Foucault, 1997, p. 228). He became, in short, a statesman.

In this way, Clovis I exemplifies what Max Weber had described as the process of routinization, when a charismatic leader is able to consolidate power and institute a regime that relies increasingly on rational principles, rather than the mystifying power of the extraordinary leader (1947, pp. 363–373). That is to say, that during such a transition, the extraordinary becomes ordinary, domesticated

---

2 The Carolingian dynasty that succeeded the Merovingians had made a fascinating distinction, apparently, arguing that there were three types of rulers: just kings (which they claimed to be), unjust kings (tyrants), and useless kings (which they claimed the last Merovingian kings to have been) (Geary, 1988, p. 224). This is a distinction of some utility for leadership studies.

3 Foucault (1997) reports that Henri de Boulainvilliers construed things differently. De Boulainvilliers concluded that Clovis may have begun as a seasonal war leader with limited authority. But inasmuch as he kept finding excuses to wage war year-after-year, eventually he grew into being king in perpetuity (p. 152). Clovis treated war less as a disruption, the affair of a season, and more as a way of life, a perennial condition (p. 156). But then Foucault also says the following: "I am obviously not saying that what Boulainvilliers said is true" (p. 163). Nevertheless, Clovis did straddle two periods, in one of which his authority was more limited by tradition and the will of the people (Canning, 1996, p. 23).

for the purposes of longevity. Attila the Hun, by comparison, failed spectacularly at this (Heather, 2006, pp. 360 & 435). His impressive empire collapsed soon after he died. To be fair, charismatic leaders come and go. Few are able to secure a civic order that endures in perpetuity. (At one point, Alaric II controlled a region larger than Clovis ever did, but he couldn't secure it.) Gaining the realm was only part of what made Clovis notable, beginning at the age of 15 with only a few hundred warriors. Others had done much the same thing during their lifetime, even though it was still a remarkable feat. What makes Clovis truly remarkable is the fact that he made that subsequent transition to stability, and he appears to have done so intentionally. Gaining power and keeping it are two different things (Gati, 2020, p. 172).

Obviously, one does not routinize authority in isolation (see Weber, 1947, p. 367). The leader has to rely on others to craft and manage the resulting system. Clovis relied on his military leaders to secure the border and keep the peace. He relied on professional experts in the law to administer justice. He relied on wealthy landowners to generate wealth. He relied on bishops to unify the church. Unlike Hasan of Morocco, he was able to put in place a structure that did not require him personally to prove his charisma over and over again.

Archetypal psychology tells of the hero's quest, when a young man takes up the sword and shield and enters the dark heart of the forest seeking dragons to slay. Such a figure craves adventure and acclaim. We might say that he is possessed of a questing spirit. Certainly, he exhibits ambition. Nevertheless, the story ends with the older and wiser protagonist returning and giving back to his people, becoming less of a spectacle and more of a generative provider, one who presides. In this sense, the biography of Clovis I describes such a narrative arc. I disagree with Weber to this extent, however (1947, p. 364): it is not the case that at some point the leader necessarily *loses* his charisma or ambition, such that he had it previously and doesn't any longer; instead, in my opinion, he channels that charisma or ambition toward a consolidation or solidification of his gains. He will have matured.

Looking at the historical record, the task of routinization might fall to a successor. Julius Caesar needed an Augustus. Lenin apparently needed a Stalin. The same task might fall to subordinates. We do not know enough to explain the process by which Clovis routinized his charisma, except that he did delegate responsibility to so-called experts. Charisma had done its work, but now a different side of leadership was required. Some might squabble that administration (routinization) is not leadership; it's management. But I don't find that distinction to be of much use, despite a substantial literature where writers feel the need to draw a bright line between leadership and management. I have never found the distinction helpful. Leaders sometimes manage. Managers sometimes lead. The primary lesson I take away about Clovis was that he understood the distinction. He knew when to quest and when to settle in, when to rise up and do battle, and when to secure what he had obtained. I consider that awareness on his part paramount, a matter of adroit timing, a willingness to transition away from what had won him the realm in the first place toward what would hold the realm in perpetuity.

Horvath (2020) argues that charisma is to be differentiated from the Greek word *charis*. *Charis* describes each object in its perfected form, good, harmonious with its environment (p. 18). Because of its perfected status, it would not require change. Charisma, on the other hand, would seem to denote an excess, an abundance, an overflow of energy requiring everything around the leader to make accommodations (p. 19). Something in the leader disrupts the harmonious whole and unsettles the prevailing order. Horvath goes on to point out that to alter, to transform in this disturbing manner, is not the same thing as to hybridize, to blend together, which is a way of preserving two things alongside one another (p. 20). And this, one could argue, is what Clovis did. I would respond to Horvath that Clovis sought to restore order after things had already begun falling apart. He was – in a manner of speaking – supplying the impetus to regain that harmony or *charis* which was being squandered.

Camil Roman (2020) takes a different approach when analyzing charisma, characterizing charisma as an irruption from beyond, an incursion, as it were, from the divine pole of existence into our very human world (p. 37). It is a holy response to human failings. As human institutions gradually drift toward human authority or (worse) faceless, bureaucratic authority – a tendency that Weber famously laments – the gods assert themselves by means of a re-enchantment in the person of the leader (p. 39). Scholars today, and especially positivists, cannot accept such an interpretation. So, they must construct some other kind of explanation for the same phenomenon. They talk about superstition and image-building and manipulation (pp. 41–45). For them, a charismatic leader is little more than a trickster. They contend that charismatic leaders are putting on an act, playing a part in a civic drama, such that any reference to the divine and mythology turns out to be folly or a ruse and therefore fundamentally irrational. The author Roman seeks to take seriously the divine pole of reality and accept the judgment of those who consider charisma to be a gift from the gods.

John O'Brien (2020) indicates that, to some extent, Plato would concur with this assessment. In the *Statesman*, writes O'Brien, Plato appeared to be stating that in the absence of good leaders, you require good laws. The problem is that laws have a tendency to thwart good leadership (p. 102f). In other words, the human response to disorder (i.e., law) is better than bad leadership or no leadership, except that it also frustrates the emergence of good leadership, which would ultimately be better even than the authority of laws. As with Roman's assessment, humanity encloses around itself an order that keeps the community together, but it encloses itself against the divine, and at some point, the people will react to these occasional irruptions from beyond. The bearer of that divine mandate, that force seeking to crack open a closed society, is the charismatic leader.

These authors, including Horvath, Roman, and O'Brien, struggle in their recent compilation about charismatic leadership to make a distinction, therefore, between authentic charisma and fake charisma (2020). Included in that volume are contemporary studies of Greece, Latin America, France, Italy, and Hungary (with glancing remarks about the United States and Great Britain). If this distinction is at all useful, they ask, then how can we use it to detect when charisma is indeed fake? Fortunately, their efforts do not pertain directly to the leadership of Clovis, who enjoys the distance of centuries. Yet writers today who reject the possibility of a "genuine" charisma will be forced to explain the leadership of Clovis in retrospect.

Many writers have noted the relationship between periods of crisis, on the one hand, and the search for a charismatic leader to save the day, on the other. Behind this apparent relationship there is often an unspoken presupposition that the crisis *causes* the rise of the leader, propelling candidates forward in order to fix things. As noted recently, "In times of permanent liminality, the need for a leader is much more compelling than in normal times" (Ruiz et al., 2020, p. 151). Charismatic leadership is believed to be a response to the crisis, a remedy. The people fear disorder and hope that the leader will prevail against it. Not a few demagogues have tried to make such an argument. They might go so far as to fabricate a crisis simply to generate demand for their special ministrations. But in any case, the idea is that the one brings about the other. To be sure, I have said such a thing in these very pages, even though it exemplifies the logical fallacy known as *post hoc ergo propter hoc*.

For just a moment, however, I would like to offer a different image. In order to do so, I draw inspiration from the work of Michel Serres and primarily from a book titled *Genesis* (University of Michigan Press, 1995). Serres sets forth a different image, one in which the background condition, the abiding reality, is always and everywhere noise, chaos, violence – turbulence, a perpetual churning, rank anarchy, far beyond our comprehending. What we see as order is the exception, an intermittence, like a brief and happy exception, fragile and ultimately doomed – shallow islands in a choppy sea. According to this image, periods of liminality are all alike because at such times we encounter the truth of our existence in the raw. We are returned to a paramount reality that never ends. In such moments, we can no longer forget what we try so hard to ignore (our *anamnesis*). The search for order – whether by this we mean health or music or national security – looks a lot like a desperate attempt to remain fugitives from our fate, to erect something that can keep us dancing a bit longer, an attempt (in other words) to extend life and all that it means to us for as long as possible, before the Furies come to reclaim it and drag us all away.

Seen in this light, all liminal epochs would be the same. What changes as history is the human *bricolage*, the ingenuity that manifests as Home and Empire and Civilization. The same haunting experience, equivalent across the centuries, is what revivifies us anew, not unlike a wayfarer trapped in quicksand flailing and lunging to stay atop the morass.

The strange thing is that once upon a time the thinking was to build a solid foundation, a permanent structure to withstand, strong and durable, like a castle wall. Only after the passage of time (though intimated by the Greeks and Taoists) did we learn that the solid structures do collapse. They erode and stifle and arrest the very animation that we had been hoping to sustain. In the name of order, they squelch the spirit that inspired them. They become magnificent tombs. Instead, we need open systems, living structures that continuously draw from the spirit. In this sense, the charismatic leader is less of a response to crisis (liminality) and more of a response to the proven inadequacy of an outdated order. Charisma is evidence of a restoration of the spirit. Charisma therefore is the irruption of life itself against the brittle armory that promised to protect what it ultimately turned out to be strangling. Followers see it in the leader. They are attracted to it because it evokes the residual *eros* in each of us. It promises a renewal of the vigor that drove us out of the womb and launched us merrily into the dark heart of the forest as children. Charisma is an act of defiance against the metaphysical noise out there, dedicated to wiping us out, yes, but it is also a reprise of the melody we fear we may have lost by becoming (how should I put it?) domesticated, sequestered for our own good in a dank prison of our own making.

We are ourselves chaotic things, upthrust from the bosom of darkness to describe a beautiful arc. Charisma reminds us of this.

References

Canning, J. (1996). *A history of medieval political thought, 300–1450*. Routledge.

Foucault, M. (1997). *"Society must be defended": Lectures at the College de France, 1975–76* (D. Macey, trans.). Picador.

Gati, D. (2020). "The failure of democracy in Italy: From Berlusconi to Salvini." In Horvath, A., Szakolczai, A. & Marangudakis, M. (eds.). *Modern leaders: Between charisma and trickery* (ch. 9). Routledge.

Geary, P. (1988). *Before France and Germany: The creation and transformation of the Merovingian world*. Oxford University Press.

Geertz, C. (1977). "Centers, kings, and charisma: Reflections on the symbolics of power." In Ben-David, J. & Clark, T.N. (eds.). *Culture and its creators: Essays in honor of Edward Shills* (ch. 7). University of Chicago Press.

Goosmann, E. (2012). "The long-haired kings of the Franks: 'Like so many Samsons?'" *Early Medieval Europe. 20*(3): 233–259.

Haun, J. (2013, May). "A new system of power: The Franks and the Catholic church in post-Roman Gaul." (Doctoral dissertation. University of Texas at Arlington).

Heather, P. (2006). *The fall of the Roman Empire: A new history of Rome and the Barbarians*. Oxford University Press.

Horvath, A. (2020). "Beyond charisma: Catacombing sensual governance by painful breaking of human ties." In Horvath, A., Szakolczai, A. & Marangudakis, M. (eds.). *Modern leaders: Between charisma and trickery* (ch. 1). Routledge.

O'Brien, J. (2020). "Plato's *Statesman*: Defending *phronesis* from coding." In Horvath, A., Szakolczai, A. & Marangudakis, M. (eds.). *Modern leaders: Between charisma and trickery* (ch. 5). Routledge.

Roman, C.F. (2020). "Charisma: From divine gift to the democratic leader-shop." In Horvath, A., Szakolczai, A. & Marangudakis, M. (eds.). *Modern leaders: Between charisma and trickery* (ch. 2). Routledge.

Ruiz, O., Jardim, F. & Teixeira, A. (2020). "The trickster logic in Latin America: Leadership in Argentina and Brazil." In Horvath, A., Szakolczai, A. & Marangudakis, M. (eds.). *Modern leaders: Between charisma and trickery* (ch. 7). Routledge.

Serres, M. (1995). *Genesis: Studies in literature and science* (revised ed., G. James & J. Nielson, trans.). University of Michigan Press.

Weber, M. (1947). *The theory of social and economic organization* (A.M. Henderson & T. Parsons, trans.). Free Press.

3

BENEATH THE LAYER OF CHIEFTAINS AND KINGS

At any given moment in time, a complex society requires leadership of some sort at every level. It would be a distortion of reality to imagine that the only leader is the person at the top of the hierarchy – such as the prince or mayor or CEO. Leadership permeates and cascades down through layers; this is true despite the tendency of journalists and historians to focus on the drama at the upper echelons. Students of leadership must not forget that while one individual human being might exert a disproportionate influence – by virtue of power or status, for example – the entire rest of the social structure pulsates with mutual (and sometimes competing) influence (see Foucault, 1997, p. 29). Thus, during the rise of Clovis, there was a lot more leadership going on. For some 30 years within the region of Gaul, he was certainly the most eminent leader in the midst of many more, including subordinates and rivals and successors. In fact, if we are interested in the leadership of a Clovis, we should probably also study the constellation of forces within which he worked – not (I might add) in order to diminish his significance so much as to appreciate his significance *in context*.

For instance, Clovis entered onto a social scene that was already changing, shifting away from the model that had governed Gaul for centuries. One empire was in the process of declining, as we said, but that process was happening slowly. And its influence over Gaul never completely disappeared. At the same time, barbarian contenders struggled for dominance, all within a larger state of flux throughout Europe. We can see multiple ethnic groups and multiple cultures jostling for a place. Some would increase, some would decrease, and some would blend or merge together. Furthermore, whereas Clovis became the paramount figure of his times, social life in Gaul constellated around different pursuits, including law, local politics, commerce, education, and religion, each of which required degrees of leadership. Clovis was not willing or able to manage all these simultaneously. In

DOI: 10.4324/9781003297802-3

many of these pursuits, Clovis himself was nearly inconsequential. At least much of what he did had no immediate effect on daily life.

In summary, as one historian puts it, "The population of Clovis's kingdom was complex and heterogeneous in its social, cultural, and economic traditions" (Geary, 1988, p. 95).

Foucault notices that eventually historians shift their attention away from eminent leaders and dramatic encounters at the top of the hierarchy, opting instead for the rhythms of ordinary life, the ebb and flow of society (1997, p. 134). This shift was justified in part as an attempt to complement the more conventional tales of conquest and large-scale drama. But Foucault asserts that doing so was also a kind of ideological colonization of the profession on behalf of a distinct social class. In other words, those who wanted to justify the importance of the aristocracy hoped to get away from celebrating the exploits of the king, such as Clovis, by emphasizing that it was *their* social class (and not Clovis) who made society function and kept it going while kings waged their battles and plotted to seduce or assassinate one another. In short, aristocrats wanted to be able to argue that they were the real heroes in the founding story (p. 136). Needless to say, other social classes would later try to accomplish the same thing (see Foucault, 1997, ch. 10).[1] First, though, they each had to delegitimize the king's sovereignty by showing that it was nothing more than an unseemly power grab. Then, they had to change the topic of the conversation by looking closely at mundane matters, such as agriculture, local law enforcement, patronage of the arts, and the like. What was happening at the top, they said, had little consequence down below. This at least was apparently the strategy.[2]

If this is indeed the case, they were assisted by the fact that the times they were hoping to describe were in turmoil. The established order had been in a state of flux, such that one could construe authority in different ways, depending on the chosen vantage point. Edward Shils offers a simple schema regarding the structure of society by referring to a center and its periphery (1961). In stable regimes, there would be an elite clustered around what he calls a central value system – a system that would have been largely nonconscious and treated as sacred. Other values and even entire value systems of a lesser status certainly existed, but they were marginal, secondary, or, in his words, "peripheral" to the regime. This

1 Foucault alleges that some historians want to make the claim that Clovis allied himself with the Gallic underclass, the indigenous peoples over whom he ruled, and stood with them *against* the Frankish warriors who had put Clovis on the throne to begin with – a notion that strains credulity (1997, p. 153).

2 This rhetorical tactic actually fit traditional norms of Roman society by which local deliberation about local issues forged men worthy of civilization. Roman citizens were always meant to be more than subjects, so a degree of autonomy was considered an expression of Roman values (Heather, 2006, p. 38). For a long time, the Roman Empire had exalted the primacy of local politics for local leaders, so that a broad loyalty to Rome was in actual practice often obscured by concerns over regional issues (Brown, 1971, p. 129).

central value system necessarily justifies the authority of that elite, including both the institutions and rules that governed society; an elite and its value system could not afford to be seen at cross-purposes. Stability relied on this arrangement coming down to the present by means of tradition, so that one could take for granted who would be dominant from one generation to the next.

Shils (1961) notes that most folks probably were somewhat removed from the particulars of that value system. Given their remoteness from the corridors of power, they may not have been bound to it formally. They might not even have known much about it. They operated within their own system which he calls "pockets of approximate independence." Needless to say, of course, they were not permitted to contradict the central value system, the core, for that would have been treason. Still, they could often carry on with their conventional lives. One reason for this was the sheer size and complexity of the empire; the central authorities could not micromanage every village and hamlet (Heather, 2006, p. 107f) – nor did they want to, as long as everybody (except perhaps the church) paid their taxes.

What the Franks encountered, however, was anything but a stable system. The territory of Gaul had been operating for a long time with a Roman center and various minor peripheral pockets scattered across the countryside. Clovis may have hoped to convince everyone to accept him as a simple replacement, a barbarian Caesar at the center, or as the next imperial authority in a long line of them, but the times would have made that difficult. Even so, these pockets likely persisted as before. Shils writes, "As long as societies were loosely coordinated, as long as authority lacked the means of intensive control and as long as much economic life of the society was carried on outside any market or almost exclusively in local markets, the central value system invariably became attenuated in the outlying reaches" (1961, p. 124). Only later, as the Franks solidified their position and the church grew in its influence, would the incompatibilities, such as they were, create intolerable tensions needing to be resolved somehow. Thus, for a long time, these pockets could persist no matter who took the throne. Such was the situation under Clovis. "Feudalism" was one word for the resolution between center and periphery that emerged only after Clovis had long since passed away.

In 1985, Raymond van Dam published an extensive study of these underlayers of the social hierarchy in a book titled *Leadership and Community in Late Antiquity Gaul*. In that book, he analyzes society during the reign of Clovis while barely mentioning him by name – which is his central point: namely, that there was other leadership going on. It will be my purpose in this section to summarize some of his findings.

Admittedly, van Dam does at a smaller magnitude what most historians do at a larger one; i.e., he identifies and isolates exemplary individuals such as Martin of Tours and Gregory of Tours and tells their story, much in the same way that we just did about Clovis. Nevertheless, van Dam intentionally uses these historical figures to tell a tale that extends beyond mere biography. As he does so, he makes general observations and describes broader patterns in the social life of that era.

Part of van Dam's message is that, regardless of what was happening in the power struggles going back and forth between aspirants for a throne – where one can track the narrative arc involving outsized personalities such as Anastasius the Byzantine emperor; Theodoric, king of the Ostrogoths and lord of the Apennine Peninsula; and Alaric II, king of the Visigoths and lord of the Iberian Peninsula – local communities continued to function. Cities needed administration. Religions vied for allegiance. Wealthy and accomplished young men rose to positions of responsibility. Life went on pretty much as it had before. And to the extent that communal life was also changing, as it often does, these crosscurrents took place below the surface and in many cases totally independent from the power struggles at the top (see also Geary, 1988). Or, we can adopt Shils' imagery of the center and periphery. What van Dam then does in his book is explain where these less-celebrated trends and tendencies ultimately intersect with the grand narrative about Clovis, contributing substantially to the so-called Dark Ages and ultimately to feudalism.

In his analysis, the author makes a number of critical distinctions. First, he differentiates nominal leaders from actual leaders. Whereas one person might enjoy a position or the prestige that we associate with leadership, such as Clovis as king, somebody else we barely notice might be driving the changes that we see. Another distinction that he makes is between civic leadership and religious leadership – a distinction that will increasingly blur throughout Gaul, despite being a distinction that Clovis himself was scrupulous to preserve. Yet another distinction separates the very top (or center) of the social hierarchy from a distributed aristocracy, in a variation on elite theory popularized by a string of Italian sociologists and punctuated by Roberto Michels in his Iron Law of Oligarchy – the idea that every complex society separates into elites and masses (Levine, 1995, ch. 11). There had been an elite under Roman rule in antiquity. There was also an elite under a system of feudalism in the Middle Ages. Van Dam wanted the reader to notice how that elite stratum negotiated the uncertainty that arose during the transition from one epoch to the other. The elite managed to survive, but only by adapting to changing circumstances. This, he would argue, is the real story.[3]

Patrick Geary explained in 1988 that, under the Romans, the basic structure of Gaul's economy had been based on large, rural, agricultural estates, governed privately by elite families in a local aristocracy (1988, p. 7; see generally pp. 96–103). He writes, "Power over the people was held by the great landowners, who were

---

3 Geary writes that "the Gallo-Roman aristocracy comprised an independent, self-perpetuating elite whose social status and political power was based on their ancestry, inherited wealth, and special status under law" (1988, p. 110). Paul Fouracre (2022) observes, however, that under Clovis this adaptable elite learned to affiliate with the Roman Catholic Church and maintain some kind of relationship with the king (p. 38).

the real authority" (1988, p. 93; see Brown, 1971, p. 37). Clearly, representatives of the empire, both soldiers and bureaucrats, had for a long time tended to dominate within their spheres, but as the Roman system disintegrated, these institutions evaporated, leaving local landowners and the church to preserve a sense of order (Heather, 2006, pp. 28 & 116). As the empire waned, however, many landholders fled these heavily taxed properties, leaving them fallow for years. Arable land was being abandoned at an alarming rate (1988, p. 37; cf. Heather, 2006, p. 112). When the regime settled later under the Franks, who adopted a different form of taxation, these neglected estates became extremely attractive to those who were sufficiently enterprising (1988, p. 96). Nevertheless, among the incoming Franks, farming had little prestige, except perhaps the husbandry of cattle (1988, p. 46). In this vacuum, local leaders found an opportunity. Clovis had learned from the Romans to allow local authorities to continue their leadership as before, which the landowners were only too happy to exercise (see Haun, 2013, p. 27).

These local aristocrats carried forward many of the forms and much of the content of Roman culture.[4] They were better educated, for example, and raised to value Roman ideals. Because of their local status and abilities, they served as natural brokers with central administration – whoever happened to be in charge (van Dam, 1985, p. 15). As the imperial presence from Rome formally withdrew from Gaul, they stayed (1985, p. 167). The claim is that they were in a sense the glue that kept local communities together. They were especially critical in buffer states, the regions between barbarian kingdoms, where the lines of authority were uncertain and contested, or changed back and forth as the monarchs battled for supremacy (1985, p. 204).

Some of these aristocrats tried to insulate their communities from the shocks of geopolitical upheaval, sheltering them from turbulence. A small number withdrew so much from the disarray that they and their people become like bandits, outside the law completely (1985, pp. 16–20; see Derrida, 2009). Other aristocrats jockeyed for advantage, forging alliances where they could. A few saw an opportunity to join the big dogs and try to become like emperors themselves. Throughout, though, the communities needed somebody to provide security and day-to-day justice (van Dam, 1985, p. 19), while whole armies passed across their territory like a thunderstorm. That is to say that ordinary people desired to be governed by competent, responsive authorities who stayed and got the job done, whatever that job happened to be (1985, p. 27). This had been part of the Roman structure for generations, so that folks were simply used to it and expected it (see, e.g., Heather, 2006, p. 35).

---

4 Despite having been conquered by Rome, Gallic society learned to honor Roman culture. They revered the memory of Julius Caesar. By the time of Clovis, the people of Gaul retained respect and even affection for Roman ways (van Dam, 1985, p. 174; see Heather, 2006, p. 37). Aristocrats continued to raise their children to emulate the Romans, even while the empire foundered.

Peter Heather (2006) put the case cynically:

> We might understand the participation of the landowners in the Roman system . . . as a cost-benefit equation. What it cost them was the money they paid annually into the state coffers. What they got in return was protection for the wealth on which their status was based. In the fourth century, benefit hugely outweighed cost. But . . . should the taxman become too demanding, or the state incapable of providing protection, then the loyalty of the landowning class could be up for renegotiation.
>
> *(p. 140)*[5]

This fact led van Dam to make a further distinction. Under the Romans, private authority was unlike public authority. A wealthy landowner was not necessarily expected to levy taxes or preside over assemblies. He was expected to mind his business, literally. No doubt the wealthy landowner influenced public governance – how could he not? Aristocrats since time immemorial have participated to one degree or another in civic affairs. But the landowner had a distinct social function. As the Roman infrastructure became diffuse, however, wealthy landowners had to assume some of these public functions (1985, p. 35). Nobody else was in a position to do so. Here, one recognizes the seeds of feudalism. For the time being, this arrangement, this merging of public and private authority, was an adaptation at the local level to a power vacuum. In some regions, the barbarian overlords became invested in these tasks, but not always. And as the fortunes of these overlords shifted according to the tides of war, back and forth, somebody had to ensure continuity of service. Central administration (no matter who was in charge) often found these local arrangements inconvenient, even though they usually had to rely upon them to keep the peace and sustain the flow of commerce (1985, p. 45; Ward-Perkins, 2005, p. 68). In fact, the barbarian economies were not built on commerce or trade or even large-scale agriculture. They were built for conquest and booty (see Wood, 2013, p. 25).[6]

What emerged was a rarified nobility of deputized Frankish commanders known as "counts," with a small garrison responsible for maintaining law and order in a specific locality (Geary, 1988, p. 94). Otherwise, these counts let local leaders administer the territory pretty much as they always had.

---

5 Heather also writes that when your wealth is based on land ownership, you must find a way to work with whoever exercises dominion. If a barbarian gives you a chance to hold on to your land and its revenue, while at the same time protecting you from predation, you will most certainly strike a deal (p. 422).

6 Wallace-Hadrill (1962) comments that the Franks presided over an economy they were ill-equipped to understand (p. 79). In fact, it was a recurring theme throughout Europe as the barbarian tribes kept migrating in part to find food they were not capable of cultivating for themselves (1962, p. 23ff). The Franks had the sense to let the existing system continue with a minimum of disruption.

In a development parallel to the empowerment of the wealthy landowners, the Roman Catholic Church as an institution was also struggling to establish itself in Gaul.[7] The oversight from Rome was jeopardized and eventually had to be removed completely to Constantinople. Thus, local clergy assumed greater autonomy and importance. Wood (2017) estimates that there were about 10,000 priests and bishops in Gaul (p. 66). Many saw this career field as an opportunity. One can find, as an equivalent to the local aristocracy, therefore, the emerging importance of bishops.

Whereas the local aristocracy tended to be grounded in rural landholdings, bishops tended to preside at urban centers. As cities grew during this era, the importance of bishops also grew (Wood, 2022, pp. 145 & 152, citing Rapp, *Holy Bishops in Late Antiquity*). Bishops led in different ways from the aristocracy, for they were teachers and scholars, healers and wonder workers, moral police, symbols of a unity that was otherwise lacking now that Rome had collapsed (van Dam, 1985, pp. 63–68, 72; cf. Geary, 1988, p. 33f). They relied on tactics such as mystification and what we might call emotion-mongering. They were in possession of esoteric knowledge that the masses increasingly found valuable (1985, p. 130), knowledge about what the scriptures said, for example, and how to drive out demons. As van Dam puts it, they discovered that holiness was a resource, like wealth and education. In that era, "holiness was power" (1985, p. 194). Clovis himself appears to have thought so.

The bishops (like most urbanites) had an interest in highlighting the extent to which they (and not the landed gentry) carried on the cosmopolitan sophistication and manners of ancient Rome, unlike those coarse country folks and their rustic ways (van Dam, 1985, pp. 69 & 231; Wood, 2017, p. 32). Many bishops were not originally native to Gaul in the first place, so that they preserved some sense of their identity as citizens of the world. By contrast, local gentry tended to embrace their local origins. Nevertheless, each of these types of local leader, both aristocracy and bishops, countryside and city centers, had the merit of being there among the people, not somewhere off at the imperial court or campaigning along with barbarian warlords. By and large, these local leaders were regularly immersed in the lives of ordinary folks.[8]

An important difference between the local aristocrats and their urban and religious counterparts was that bishops had some responsibility to advance the cause of the church, for example, by defining heresy and converting the pagan. Quite a few bishops were able to use this mission to enhance their own authority and to

---

7 Peter Brown notes that, for many Romans still in Gaul, about the only vestige of their Roman-ness was the Roman Catholic Church, so they clung to it more as a cultural residue of their former glory (1971, p. 126).

8 After Clovis, this pattern would change, as ambitious men gravitated toward the Merovingian court first, proving themselves and networking in order to win the privilege of being entrusted with local authority (Hen, 2022, p. 223).

spread their influence across a wider region. At the very least, it helped to solidify a community to know whom to admit and whom to expel from membership (van Dam, 1985, p. 86). In any case, their religion was not merely a local affair (1985, p. 84). This fact was in part what contributed to their stature, inasmuch as they could cite connections to a transcending ordering force beyond the local (Weber, 1921/1958, p. 109) – whether by a "transcending ordering force" they meant the Church Universal or God.

Over time, of course, history records the gradual Christianizing of Gaul. That is a story unto itself. What van Dam wants the reader to notice is that at the same time the church was gradually being transformed by the aristocrats into a kind of parallel aristocracy. The two types of local leader started to resemble one another (1985, p. 116f). He calls this "lateral mobility" (1985, p. 153; cf. Wood, 2017, p. 84; Brown, 2002) – the same prominent families fed the next generation of landowners and bishops. As we have been seeing, the line between the landed gentry and the bishops blurred (see Fouracre, 2022, p. 44).

This peculiar transition was the result of many factors, some of them demographic. When chastity became an ideal among Christians, fewer aristocrats produced offspring. Some family lines came to an end, at which point the land (and its people) frequently passed over to the church, there being no heirs (1985, p. 203; Wood, 2017, p. 97).[9] The church obtained much wealth as a result (Heather, 2006, p. 121) – wealth Clovis explicitly refused to covet. Yet, at the same time, it required managers to sustain operations, and this role (now part of the church hierarchy) was often filled by other aristocrats.[10] If they acquitted themselves favorably, they might aspire to become bishops themselves (Geary, 1988, p. 33). In

---

9 Ian Wood writes, "The Church impacted upon everything that contributed to its upkeep, which involved vast transfers of land and wealth (in Francia perhaps up to a third of the kingdom)" (2013, p. 5; Wood, 2017, p. 101, 2022). Later, Wood explains that the church had at least four types of expenditures: the bishop and his staff; other clergy distributed throughout the vicinity; poor relief (a financial burden that was not trivial and which included care for the sick, i.e., hospitals); and the construction, maintenance, and repair of church buildings (2017, ch. 9; see generally Wood, 2022, p. 54ff re: the *Quadripartum*; regarding public health and hospitals, see generally Horden, 2022, ch. 14). This includes such miscellany as paying ransoms and providing for funerals (Wood, 2017, p. 92; see also Wood, 2022, p. 70). In some instances, they had to repair city walls, lay underground pipes, and monitor contact with other cities during times of pestilence (Wood, 1994, p. 76; see Geary, 1988, p. 98). The technical term for describing the bishops' administrative and jurisdictional activities is *Bischofsherrschaft* (Wood, 2022, pp. 154–159).

10 Many landowners recognized that they were better off ceding title of the land to the church in exchange for lifetime employment and enjoyment as its managers (Wood, 2017, p. 97). One reason was that church-owned real property was not taxed (Wood, 2017, p. 102; cf. Wood, 2022, p. 162). It was not unheard of for the landowner to donate the land (earning all the spiritual merit that accrued from doing so) and then by agreement lease the land back from the church so that they would still run it (Wood, 2017, p. 100). Thus, the church accumulated land piecemeal and also drew proceeds from the leases every season as income, without having to get involved in day-to-day operations. Nevertheless, as Wood points out, this pattern of immense church holdings tended to become controversial only after Clovis had passed away (2017, p. 104).

fact, the church found talent and ambition among the aristocrats, many of whom needed an outlet for their energies. Only so many heirs were needed to run the large estates. What of the other offspring? The church was a logical place for them to look for advancement (Wood, 2022, p. 155). Further, as aristocrats took Christianity seriously, many genuinely wanted to devote themselves to its service – more so than managing farms (but see Wood, 2017, p. 110). The supply of foreigners into the clergy was also dwindling. And, as the nation Christianized over time, more and more clergy were needed. They had to come from somewhere. Aristocrats brought with them a host of useful skills, not least of which was basic literacy. As Roman influence subsided, their schools went away. In their place was a network of monastic and ecclesiastical schools (van Dam, 1985, p. 133; cf. Wood, 2013, p. 284), so the brighter students found themselves already in the bosom of the church before they even started contemplating a career.

Peter Brown in 2002 published his Menahem Stern Jerusalem Lectures as *Poverty and Leadership in the Later Roman Empire*. Even though much of the content pertained to the Byzantine Empire in the east, he did successfully address the emergence of bishops as a new kind of leader. Before the time of interest to us in this study of Clovis, bishops had claimed the authority and responsibility to care for the poor within the Christian community. As Brown points out, though, this role expanded to embrace all of the poor (but see Brown, 1971, p. 67), including those who were only temporarily beset by poverty or passing through his jurisdiction as migrants. Furthermore, the definition of poverty expanded beyond the truly destitute to include, for example, widows and orphans, no matter how wealthy they were otherwise. Not only that, but the bishops increasingly did more than distribute alms; they hosted local courts to help resolve conflicts, employed the poor to serve the church in one capacity or another, and petitioned civil authorities on behalf of their parishioners. These civil authorities were increasingly happy to let the church manage these problems so that they no longer had to do so. In order to conduct these activities, the bishops required income for themselves to cover these operations, portraying themselves as having become impoverished for Christ. In this way, the original distinction between the rich and the poor as a simple polarity became more elaborate, solidifying the bishops as leaders to be reckoned with.

As bishoprics gained in stature (and wealth), they became more desirable generally for ambitious men. Competition for these offices became fierce. Aristocrats saw this and tried to use their influence to secure positions in the church for their sons, even to the point of bribing officials (van Dam, 1985, p. 206). A bishopric was lucrative.[11] Wood (2022) estimates that there must have been fewer than 130

---

11 Many who entered this office were already wealthy, having moved laterally from successful families. When these clerics eventually passed away, many died intestate, which meant that the church obtained the rights to their substantial holdings (Wood, 2017, p. 99; see Wood, 2022, p. 28). In

of these positions altogether throughout Gaul (p. 41). It was also an appointment for life, which meant that there were few empty seats at any given time; the inventory was remarkably small. Needless to say, this fact intensified the competition when a seat came open (1985, p. 212). When a valuable commodity becomes scarce, the price goes up. As the aristocracy started to thin out, the remaining families tried to consolidate their power by intermarrying for advantage, engaging in tactical unions, which in turn created a smaller number of very powerful families that operated as a unit, countering many of the advantages of the bishops. Members of the aristocracy would then connive to place family members in certain seats of ecclesiastical power, so that many of these exalted positions (along with the accompanying shrines, relics, and cults) became de facto property of the family – which obviously had the effect of consolidating their power even further (1985, p. 207). These seats were even known at the time as *patriae sedes*, or family sees (1985, pp. 209 & 211; Geary, 1988, p. 35).[12]

In a parallel move, some families (and even some kings) skipped over the office of bishop completely in order to create their own cult, complete with relics and shrines, sponsoring writers to cast them or their forebearers as holy men (van Dam, 1985, p. 229). After all, for them, the office of bishop was only a means to an end: it was holiness itself that they sought.

The exemplary Martin of Tours had been different (see, e.g., Brown, 1971, p. 109f). Martin earned his stature through raw competence. But then, it helps to notice that he rose prior to the time of Clovis. In particular, he would set an example of a bishop who served more as a civic authority than as a priest (van Dam, 1985, ch. 6; see Geary, 1988, pp. 140–143). He was a peculiar character who fed the imagination of aristocrats who wanted to lead and now saw that they could do so from within the church. Martin also fed the imagination of bishops who found it appealing to think that they too could govern. Later then, in the days of Clovis, bishops used the example of Martin to justify their own leadership. Martin was a kind of role model for the new governing class.

Van Dam writes that Christianity shaped the aristocracy, to be sure; but, at the same time, the aristocracy shaped the church (1985, p. 141). With increasing frequency, local leadership was both/and. Not only that, but many of these hybrid leaders found themselves serving as ambassadors (1985, p. 148), mingling with some frequency among the upper echelons of society and bridging Gaul with other kingdoms. Some became even more than local leaders.

---

fact, a few wealthy bishops purportedly used their personal wealth as leverage to direct the church to select their hand-picked successor (often, a blood relative) under the threat of divesting themselves of this wealth to private interests if the church were to refuse them (Wood, 2017, p. 100).

12 It probably goes without saying that kings recognized the advantages of controlling who occupied these positions, such that they too joined the fray when seats became vacant (Wood, 1994, p. 78; van Dam, 1985, p. 218). The struggle between church and state – and, more concretely, who could select bishops (and then archbishops) – persisted throughout the Middle Ages.

Whereas some clergy joined the ranks of the cosmopolitan elite, going into the proverbial corridors of power abroad, others stayed put and expanded their local footprint to obtain increasing status as the reputation of their shrines and relics grew. Here, we see the emergence of cults that exerted a kind of gravitational pull beyond their borders. In other words, some talented and ambitious leaders went to where the power was; others established their own power where they were and brought the world to them – for example, by means of pilgrimages (see van Dam, 1985, p. 194).

The resulting fusion of aristocracies – both clergy and lay – fit the preferences of a Clovis, who had other things on his mind. He tended to defer to the experts in both law and religion, as long as they coordinated their efforts with one another and left him in a position to assert himself as needed (1985, p. 181). Bishops were all too happy to assume a dominant role where they could, grounded in Old Testament examples when prophets presumed to judge even the kings anointed by YHWH (1985, p. 197). Again, one sees the emergence of a relationship between church and state that would define the entire Middle Ages. To be sure, the system that resulted was initially confusing and messy, as local leaders competed with one another and oftentimes overlapped (1985, p. 185). Even so, Clovis sanctioned the leadership of counts and bishops, abbots, and the occasional saint (1985, p. 185). After all, as we saw earlier, Frankish kings were not customarily responsible for administering day-to-day business, especially on such a large scale (1985, p. 185; see Steenkamp, 2020, p. 25). To some extent, Clovis left them to figure it out. Yet he did expect them to figure it out. Thus, Clovis championed a period of "profound localism" (Geary, 1988, pp. 228 & 230). This I consider to be a superlative lesson.

The result was what Max Weber refers to as a "plastic dualism" between purposes, both political and economic (1921/1958, p. 78), as cities struggled to adapt themselves to a new constellation of powers.[13]

What van Dam describes had little or nothing to do with the structure of the military. This was the clear responsibility of Clovis, who had assumed the premier position since being elected by his peers. Yet even within the ranks of such a large organization, there had to be a variety of intermediate commanders. That is to say that, even within the military, there was an underlayer of leadership. For example, Clovis negotiated a number of pacts with these subordinate officers as a way of delineating authority and granting local military leaders a degree of autonomy. Helmut Reimitz (2019) refers to the resulting structure as a *militärisch*

---

13 Weber (1921/1958) examines the three most basic affiliations in occidental cities during the Middle Ages – namely, family/village, occupation/guild, and territory/administration (p. 82). It became increasingly unclear which of these determined a person's loyalties. You will notice that Weber does not include one's clan or tribe, such as the Franks, and he explains why that was the case in that epoch (pp. 100 & 103). Thus, it became increasingly possible to meld these peoples into a singular identity as Frenchmen.

konstituierten Monarchie – that is, a kind of constitutional configuration grounded in a complex web of transactions (p. 49; see generally Sarti, 2022, ch. 12).

As it happens, when Clovis passed away, the rulership at the top soon became dysfunctional. Yet the borders had been sufficiently secured during his reign that clear military leadership at the top was not urgently required. In the meantime, the rest of the domain's leadership, populated by this non-Frankish elite, kept things going, so that we might say that, as a group, they deserve considerable credit for the longevity of the Merovingian dynasty (Glassman, 2017, p. 1490; Wallace-Hadrill, 1962, p. 75).

A critic of van Dam might be excused for thinking that he was painting a grim picture of local leaders as grasping, even manipulative creatures, positioning themselves to exploit circumstances out of self-interest or fanaticism.[14] Undoubtedly, many of them were acquisitive. Others were possibly overzealous for their faith. And a smaller number probably used the credulity of the people at that time as a cover for their own greed, capitalizing on widespread superstition (see, e.g., Wood, 2013, p. 58). Given the scarcity of first-person accounts from that era, the bias of early historians, and what we know about human nature generally, it would be remarkable if none of the local leaders succumbed to vice or immoderate devotion. Nevertheless, van Dam stops short of making blanket accusations against them as a class. One could as easily indict Clovis himself for much worse. Taking a giant step back, we might be advised to come away thinking that any durable social system will always involve assorted human failings. Perhaps the proper question ought to be stated as follows: how does a complex system account in a sustainable fashion for these failings?

One could ask a different question, however, based on the same basic evidence, which has to do with the causal factors that led to feudalism and the Dark Ages (without presupposing that feudalism and the Dark Ages were altogether bad things).[15] Did the rise of the Roman Catholic Church, for example, consign

---

14 Wood cites historians such as Joseph Emmanuel Sieyès who took the position that the substance of society was preserved at an even lower level, known subsequently as the third estate. This level was made up of peasants, craftsmen, and laborers, such that both the aristocrats and the bishops were little more than parasites (2013, p. 50; see Graceffa, 2022, p. 58) – clearly, an opinion that van Dam disputes. Perhaps it is fair to say that a thorough account would credit each social class in turn.

15 Wood (2017) points out that Clovis ushered in a period that was to see the least large-scale military activity "than in any other period of European history" – suggesting that the epithet "Dark" might be a misnomer (p. 82). It was a relatively peaceful time . . . at least in Gaul (but see Wood, 1994, p. 93). Furthermore, the educated class was by all accounts just as intelligent and enterprising as any other. The only difference was how they chose to use their time and energies. That is, either they valued the church, theology, and the pursuit of holiness or they applied themselves to agriculture and commerce, seeing these pursuits as somehow more important than trade, the arts, or the rudiments of science. It is therefore a reflection of our own prejudice to label their epoch the Dark Ages (Wood, 2017, p. 117). Leaders in that era had priorities different from our own. Ian Wood has recently pointed out that the economy shifted measurably during this time, primarily toward enriching the church, but that fact did not necessarily signify a deterioration (2022, p. 26).

France to centuries of squalid regression from the grandeur that was Rome? Was this time period evidence that religion is indeed the opiate of the masses? Or was it the fault of the conniving aristocrats populating the ranks of the elite in order to keep themselves and their offspring afloat? That is to say, are we witness here to a classic example of class struggle? Or, for that matter, did the way of the barbarian, exemplified by Clovis and his heirs, condemn Europe to this regrettable passage? Historians differ.

A more neutral rendering might indicate that Vilfredo Pareto was essentially correct: history records the perpetual circulation of elites, with one dominant class displacing another – sometimes abruptly, as in 1789, and sometimes in slow motion; sometimes without too much disruption, and sometimes accompanied by extensive violence (Taylor, 2004, p. 34; see generally Pareto, 1991).

To a great extent, much depends on what the reader considers so worthy about the Roman Empire to begin with. By some accounts, the twilight of that civilization – its rump or remainder, as it were – was a time of oppressive, misguided, corrupt, and flabby maladministration. Maybe the Romans simply squandered their birthright and guaranteed the onset of a long and devastating reckoning. In brief, it would seem that there is plenty of blame to go around. We cannot conclude that van Dam was trying to resolve these issues about the decline and fall of Rome, a topic which is too vast and intricate by far. Yet he was offering a window into the layer of leadership that historians (and leadership scholars) can be tempted to overlook when they scrutinize the past.

We end by agreeing with Michel Foucault: "The feudal nobility of the Middle Ages was, at bottom, no more than a mixture of three aristocracies, and it established itself as a new aristocracy that exercised a relationship of domination over people who were themselves a mixture of Gaulish tributaries, Roman clients, and German subjects" (1997, p. 230).

References

Brown, P. (2002). *Poverty and leadership in the later Roman Empire.* University Press of New England.

Brown, P. (1971). *The world of Late Antiquity, AD 150–750.* Thames & Hudson, Ltd.

Derrida, J. (2009). *The beast and the sovereign* (vol. 1, G. Bennington, trans.). University of Chicago Press.

Ward-Perkins (2005) disputes this claim and draws from considerable archeological evidence that indeed the living conditions throughout Western Europe were deteriorating. A complex economy, with all its material comforts, evaporated, reducing the region to a primitive state (chs. 5 & 7). Commerce faltered, household goods became crude, architecture had to be radically simplified, literacy was less widespread, and the population in general shrank. He insists that historians must record the overall decline, if for no other reason than to remind us today that things can get worse. He writes, "Romans before the fall were as certain as we are today that their world would continue for ever substantially unchanged. They were wrong" (p. 183).

Foucault, M. (1997). *"Society must be defended": Lectures at the College de France, 1975–76* (D. Macey, trans.). Picador.

Fouracre, P. (2022). "From Gaul to Francia: The impact of the Merovingians." In Effros, B. & Moreira, I. (eds.). *The Oxford handbook of the Merovingian world* (ch. 2). Oxford University Press.

Geary, P. (1988). *Before France and Germany: The creation and transformation of the Merovingian world.* Oxford University Press.

Glassman, R. (2017). *The origins of democracy in tribes, city-states, and nation-states* (vol. I). Springer.

Graceffa, A. (2022). "Writing the history of Merovingian Gaul." In Effros, B. & Moreira, I. (eds.). *The Oxford handbook of the Merovingian world* (ch. 3). Oxford University Press.

Haun, J. (2013, May). "A new system of power: The Franks and the Catholic church in post-Roman Gaul." (Doctoral dissertation. University of Texas at Arlington).

Heather, P. (2006). *The fall of the Roman Empire: A new history of Rome and the Barbarians.* Oxford University Press.

Hen, Y. (2022). "The Merovingian polity: A network of courts and courtiers." In Effros, B. & Moreira, I. (eds.). *The Oxford handbook of the Merovingian world* (ch. 10). Oxford University Press.

Horden, P. (2022). "Public health, hospitals, and charity." In Effros, B. & Moreira, I. (eds.). *The Oxford handbook of the Merovingian world* (ch. 14). Oxford University Press.

Levine, D. (1995). *Visions of the sociological tradition.* University of Chicago Press.

Pareto, V. (1991). *The rise and fall of elites: An application of theoretical sociology.* Transaction Publishers.

Reimitz, H. (2019). "*Pax inter utramque gentum*: The Merovingians, Byzantium and the history of Frankish identity." In Esders, S., Fox, Y., Hen, Y. & Sarti, L. (eds.). *East and West in the Early Middle Ages: The Merovingian kingdoms in Mediterranean perspective* (ch. 3). Cambridge University Press.

Sarti, L. (2022). "The military and its role in Merovingian society." In Effros, B. & Moreira, I. (eds.). *The Oxford handbook of the Merovingian world* (ch. 12). Oxford University Press.

Shils, E. (1961). "Centre and periphery." In Polanyi Festschrift Committee (eds.). *The logic of personal knowledge: Essays presented to Michael Polanyi* (pp. 117–130). Routledge & Kegan Paul.

Steenkamp, J.-B. (2020). *Time to lead: Lessons for today's leaders from bold decisions that changed history.* Fast Company.

Taylor, C. (2004). *Modern social imaginaries.* Duke University Press.

van Dam, R. (1985). *Leadership and community in late antique Gaul.* University of California Press.

Wallace-Hadrill, J.M. (1962). *The barbarian west, AD 400–1000: The Early Middle Ages.* Harper Torchbook.

Ward-Perkins, B. (2005). *The fall of Rome and the end of civilization.* Oxford University Press.

Weber, M. (1921/1958). *The city* (D. Martindale & G. Neuwirth, trans.). Free Press.

Wood, I. (2022). *The Christian economy in the early Medieval West: Towards a temple society.* Punctum Books.

Wood, I. (2017). *The transformation of the Roman west.* Arc Humanities Press.

Wood, I. (2013). *The modern origins of the early Middle Ages.* Oxford University Press.

Wood, I. (1994). *The Merovingian kingdoms, 450–751.* Longman.

4

INTERPRETING THE PAST

The *longue durée*: civilizations, plural

The period being described in these pages demonstrates that civilizations wax and wane and sometimes disappear altogether, their remnants lost and forgotten. Often, two civilizations clash against one another. When they clash, occasionally one of them wins outright. But then two civilizations also sometimes learn to reside alongside one another, for example, to facilitate trade. And in a few instances, civilization A and civilization B blend or merge, becoming some third thing, a civilization C. What interests me in the following pages are the interstices, the spaces and times of in-betweenness, also known as liminality or (to borrow a term from Eric Voegelin) "the Metaxy," where the sway of empires has become tenuous, and nobody can say for certain how things will turn out. The collapse of the Roman Empire in Late Antiquity was one such period.

In the grand sweep of history, certain epochs signal significant change after hundreds of years of continuity and across millions of square miles. Participants themselves may not be able to recognize the precise moment when this happens, or even that it is happening at all. The process can be slow and nearly imperceptible, or swift and convulsive. Civilizations can die with a bang or a whimper. Additionally, credit and blame for these transformations are largely systemic and nobody's personal fault. There would have to be many contributing factors. The climate shifts, volcanoes erupt, deltas flood, technology rewards the bold, economies fluctuate, and pandemics lurk in centers of populations. How then to frame the epoch of interest to us during the reign of Clovis within the enduring context known as the *longue durée* (Braudel, 1980)? To what extent is the leadership of Clovis singular?

DOI: 10.4324/9781003297802-4

I am deeply indebted to Ian Wood, emeritus professor of early medieval history, University of Leeds, who pointed out:

> At any one time there will always be one or more discourses that dominate the way in which the past is being read. It is, therefore, not just the interpretation of individual events that should constantly be held up to scrutiny: so too should the more general discourse in which the interpretation is situated.
>
> *(2013, p. 329)*

In his magisterial work titled *The Modern Origins of the Early Middle Ages* (2013), Wood traces the history of those who wrote about the history of these events pertaining to Clovis. Part of his purpose is to show that it is often the case that writers themselves, many centuries after the fact, worked within a context that in turn influenced how they judge the evidence. Is the author French, German, or Italian? Is he or she a Christian? (More specifically, is she or he a Roman Catholic?) What was happening at the time the author was working on his or her studies? Had there been a war recently? Who served as the author's mentors? What were the standards at the time for scholarship? Had there been any recent discoveries that required fresh interpretation? The bias can be implicit and inadvertent. Furthermore, although Wood does not express it this bluntly (though Foucault does): in some instances, historians set out to distort history for the sake of partisan gains (1997, pp. 172 & 189).

We might notice that it is not only scholars who have a stake in these interpretations. Politicians and rulers want to find justification in antiquity for their leadership. The Hapsburgs, Bourbons, Napoleon, and the Nazis aspired to claim Clovis as a predecessor (Wood, 2013, pp. 53 & 81). But then so do those who are more democratically inclined, who regard the Franks as freedom-loving and inclined by tradition to limited governance and self-rule (e.g., Wood, 2013, pp. 12 & 41) – a position dismissed by Edward Gibbon, who regarded the entire era as a triumph of barbarism and religious fanatics (Wood, 2013, pp. 49 & 71).

Foucault (1997) notes that historians *during* the Middle Ages regarded history as continuous and unbroken from the time of the Roman Empire right through Christianized feudalism in one long sequence of events (p. 68f; see Wood, 2017, p. 6). It was only later that historians paid any attention to the disruptions of interest to us here. That is, these later historians decided in retrospect that the times could be interpreted through *multiple* histories; e.g., as the decline and fall of Rome, as the migration of the barbarians, as the rise of the Christian church, and so on (Foucault, 1997, pp. 69, 179, 189). Some saw the Romans as oppressors; others saw the barbarians as oppressors; a few saw the wealthy landowner as an oppressor (Wood, 2017, p. 4). In other words, there could be different lenses through which to study the same era. In fact, says Foucault, historians are finally taking a fresh interest in the fate of those who could be said to have "lost," the dispossessed and marginalized (Foucault, 1997, p. 71), i.e., those who were sub-jugated or driven out of their homeland. What happened to them? How did they live? Much depends on where the historian's sympathies lie.

Fortunately, with regard to leadership scholars and their sympathies, I am anticipated by Suze Wilson (2016), who has begun this process of tracking comparable influences on our work. Today, students of leadership in the twenty-first century occupy a unique position, having the benefit of all this prior research, plus widespread access to knowledge and opinion on the Internet, in an international community of scholars that can communicate more readily than was previously possible. This does not discount the lingering effects of nationality, race, gender, and other factors on an individual's unique interests. Furthermore, as the news cycle draws attention to unfolding events, such as the global war on terror, the ambiguous legacy of Arab Spring, and increasing academic reliance on critical theory, postmodernism, and identity politics, the uses and abuses to which the distant past can be put will change over time – as Wood acknowledges (2013, ch. 16). Still, current events recurrently make a history of these founding stories about Clovis relevant.

More specifically, leadership studies have transitioned away from versions of the Great Man Theory popularized by Thomas Carlyle toward more inclusive or distributed models of leadership. We have become less fixated on the tales of heroes and outsized personalities. Nevertheless, as the literature shows, time and time again, leadership studies still tend to feature the importance of individual agency, as opposed to economic forces, system dynamics, and other broader (or at least impersonal) explanations. We continue to use the lens of what individual human beings have done and can still do. And to be fair, some historical figures did exert a disproportionate influence on their times. Whether that alone makes them "great" is less clear.

It is not as though scholars face a stark, binary choice. There is room for both/and thinking. We can acknowledge the significance of systemic or structural features, without ignoring the salience of individual exertions. Any complete understanding of leadership will rely on both (see generally Harter, 2020). In addition, an astute observer can recognize leadership at many levels, ranging from the very top (e.g., kings, presidents, and CEOs) to local leadership at the bottom, at the platoon, team, or community level. Leadership occurs at nearly every magnitude in any complex organization or society, so that a focus on any one level to the exclusion of the rest will be impoverished and potentially misleading.

None of this is meant to suggest that a conscientious investigator would ignore the fact that sources on which we rely do not use other, competing lenses, whether consciously or not. To cite one example, Wood mentions the risk of misconstruing early Germanic texts as pertaining to the *volk* (as heroic, for instance), rather than to heroic individuals as exemplars (2013, p. 290). These tales were intended originally to portray the valor of extraordinary social actors. This confusion between heroes and the heroic *volk* was a mistake apparent in Nazi interpretations. There is also the allowance one must make for hagiography. For example, Gregory of Tours' account of Clovis in particular is at times doubtful; it helps to recognize what it was that Gregory was trying to accomplish in furthering the faith and, therefore, not to accept it entirely at face value as an attempt at objective history (which it wasn't).

Despite all of these cautionary notes, we are faced with a couple of additional complications regarding Clovis and the Franks.

First, we have no reason to believe that conditions prevailing in one localized geographic area applied to all of the remainder, uniformly throughout Gaul (e.g., Halsall, 2014, p. 516). What happened in Paris may not have resembled what was happening in Aquitaine. Civic order at the time would have been understandably piecemeal, or at least uneven. The entire region did not turn on an axis from one configuration to another, all at the same time. One must recognize, for example, the variation between the municipal centers and the hinterlands, a literal schema of center and periphery.

Second, Clovis arose during a time of transition, so that conditions prevailing early in his reign may not have persisted to the end of his reign. Many things were in flux. In fact, the anecdote that opens this book about the fabled vase of Soissons was selected in part to illustrate a transition from (a) the tradition of royal limits on their share of booty, in a system where the people were expected to conduct judicial functions (Wood, 2013, p. 184), to (b) a time of less accountability on the part of a king, such that Clovis could summarily execute a soldier with impunity and command his troops thereafter to respect church property.[1]

Third, conditions prevailing at one layer or stratum of society may not have prevailed at other layers. We saw this with regard to Frankish military and diplomatic supremacy, coupled with more localized Gallo-Roman leadership at the local level regarding such things as economic production. Clovis was also keen to keep his governance separate from that of the church, so that there would have been at least two parallel structures of authority. To put this succinctly, the Frankish kingdom established by Clovis was a messy amalgam of Roman, barbarian, and Christian influences (Wood, 2013, pp. 76 & 143) along a number of dimensions. Somehow, it worked.

Finally, we will remain heavily dependent on the evidence that survives, no matter what lenses we elect to use on them (e.g., Wood, 2013, p. 179). For example, one scholar points out that we know little about the lifestyle of the Celts in that part of the world. We also know little about the so-called Germanic tribes before they were encountered by Romans. And so, the first record of that people

1 Canning (1996) indicates that Clovis inherited a tradition in which he could not govern arbitrarily, as we have seen. Both Rome and the Franks had this tradition. Yet his assertions at Soissons reveal a problem in this tradition. If a leader does act arbitrarily and contrary to tradition, as Clovis apparently was attempting to do, does anyone have a right to resist? The answer was unclear, such that the question persisted into the Middle Ages (p. 25).

will have been filtered through Roman eyes (e.g., Tacitus). Not only that, but the succeeding Carolingian dynasty issued a *damnatio memoriae* in order to eradicate the record of the Merovingian regime (Wood, 1994, p. 1), making our research today all the more difficult.

From a distance, therefore, the era that witnessed the rise of the Merovingians can be interpreted in a variety of ways, depending on one's interests, training, and powers of imagination. Nevertheless, one cannot ignore the facts, such as we have them. The fact that all accounts – directly during his lifetime and indirectly for centuries to come – consider Clovis extraordinarily successful warrants closer scrutiny by leadership scholars.

Interpretations of the decline and fall of Rome

> "There is more ado to interpret interpretations than to interpret things, and more books upon books than upon any other subject; we do nothing but comment upon one another."
>
> *– de Montaigne, 1887*

Jaroslav Pelikan delivered the Rauschenbusch Lectures in 1984 and subsequently published them three years later. There, the historian reflects on the multiple lenses through which the decline and fall of Rome once recounted by Edward Gibbon can be revisited in light of subsequent research. Many luminaries have commented at one time or another on this period in history, including Adam Smith, Edmund Burke, Alexander Hamilton, Alexis de Tocqueville, Karl Marx, Oswald Spengler, and Hannah Arendt (1987, ch. 1). Nevertheless, Gibbon's version has stood out as singularly eloquent, yet skewed against the role of both the incoming barbarians and the church (1987, ch. 3). The blame, in his opinion, squarely rests with Rome itself. Rome allowed these things to happen over time. Pelikan acknowledges that Gibbon was not reductionistic about such a long and complex decline; many factors contributed. Nevertheless, the story as we know it today looks somewhat different, which is why Pelikan set about to update Gibbon.

Early Christians disagreed among themselves. Jerome, for example, regarded the decline and fall as a kind of apocalypse, not unlike the ruination of kingdoms prophesied in the Old Testament, as well as in the book of Revelation (see Pelikan, 1987, ch. 4). Rome as an empire deserved its fate, Jerome thought, as a divine judgment. Its purpose had been to restrain the dark forces of this world (i.e., the anti-Christ), which was a worthy undertaking at the time, until the church in all its splendor could rise up and assert itself. Once that originating purpose had been squandered by the Romans, the Lord had no further use for the empire, such as it was, so the church simply took possession of the structure for its own purpose. The collapse was indeed calamitous, inasmuch as it temporarily gave latitude to the anti-Christ; yet God's providential hand ensured that the church would prevail. Rome was failing in its mission, which warranted its being swept aside. The entire transition (Rome's purpose, judgment, and substitution) was governed from heaven.

By way of contrast, Gibbon keeps his focus on earthly reasons. He blames misfortune, folly, and crimes (1987, ch. 5). In his search for someone or something in this world to blame, he identifies such things as climate, geography, and weather as misfortunes. He blames superstition among the masses as folly. He blames the inadequate character of Rome's leaders, especially in the commission of outright crimes. His version of events tries to locate the various causes, of which there were many, without invoking the hand of God. Gibbon also notices that it wasn't just the accumulation of bad things, one right after the other; paradoxically, the collapse was also the ultimate consequence of its successes. That which made it great in its day is what brought about its ruin. One couldn't sustain such greatness forever. Like a character flaw depicted in some ancient tragedy, that which we admire about Rome was its undoing. It grew too big. It over-relied on its military. It cultivated opulence. It outsourced labor, both to foreigners and to slaves. And it constructed an elaborate bureaucracy that operated with unmatched efficiency, until the weight of regulation so burdened the people that it became remote and unwieldy. Finally, Rome had enjoyed an ample supply of leaders at various levels – certainly better educated and disciplined than the leaders they arrived to displace (1987, p. 88). When the leadership started to deteriorate, the system that had nurtured it and on which it relied required an infusion of fresh blood or risked collapse. Or both. According to Gibbon, apparently, the church weakened civil institutions by poaching its best leaders (1987, p. 114).

Unlike Jerome and Gibbon, Augustine seems to have found a nuanced position with regard to that fateful process. There was much to celebrate about the Roman Empire, he believed. It had done incalculably good things. It had also done very bad things. And so one could mourn its passing without renouncing its inestimable gifts (1987, ch. 9). These gifts included the law, the language, and its emergent religion.[2] That is, the church could build upon such greatness and learn from Rome's mistakes, rather than merely trusting in the disposition of the Almighty to make things right.

At the time, many observers disputed whether Rome had been replaced with something else, much as Gibbon says, or renewed and continued (as it were) under new management. Leadership was transferred to a new type of leader, primarily to the bishops, but (according to this latter point of view) they adopted the authority that had been abandoned by the pagans. Imperial authority was like a crown lying by the side of the road for someone to come along and pick up out

---

2   By language, Pelikan includes the literature of the pagans, which Western Europe could read in Latin and consult.

of the gutter. The new empire was a restoration and continuation of the old. That is something different from Jerome's interpretation that the church was a new thing, like an heir finally come in to his majority. Where this difference becomes acute is the transfer of the empire to a completely different geographical location, namely, Byzantium (to be rechristened Constantinople).[3] Was its empire the same empire or something new? This was an important question. Some viewed the decline and fall of the Roman Empire as a replacement of a pagan empire with a Christian empire, while others viewed it as a replacement of a Western empire (centered in Rome) with an Eastern one (centered in Constantinople) (Pelikan, 1987, p. 77). Few voices within the community of the faithful dared to suggest that the church should never have imperial ambitions to begin with. Those voices would increase many centuries later.

Clovis and Machiavelli's Prince

Niccolò Machiavelli was a Florentine politician and man of letters born in 1469, some thousand years after the reign of Clovis I. In 1513, Machiavelli wrote the notorious job application known today as *The Prince*. In these pages, Machiavelli uses his extensive experience in diplomacy and research to compose a guidebook for a Renaissance prince. How might one apply the lessons found in *The Prince* to what we know about Clovis – whether Machiavelli ever intended to do so or not? We know that the tensions between Clovis and his realm Francia, on the one hand, and Theodoric and his realm, on the other, continued sporadically for generations. Writing hundreds of years later, Machiavelli was especially distraught because France existed as a unified nation-state, whereas Italy as a comparable nation-state did not yet exist. Instead, it was a fractious array of city-states, as he had had reason to witness firsthand. Clovis had unified the region that would become known as France. Machiavelli explicitly hoped that Lorenzo de' Medici would do the same in Italy. *The Prince* tells the young leader how to replicate what Clovis had done ages before.

In chapter 14 of *The Prince*, Machiavelli recommends that a prospective prince "should read history, and therein study the actions of eminent men, observe how they bore themselves in war, and examine the causes of their victories and defeats, so that he may imitate the former and avoid the latter."[4] In an earlier chapter, he notes that "a wise man should ever follow the ways of great men and endeavour to imitate only such as have been most eminent" (ch. 6). He then writes, "Nothing

---

3 Clifford Ando (2008) has explained that the use of the term "Byzantine" was controversial since antiquity, inasmuch as the Byzantines understood themselves and their empire to be thoroughly Roman. It was the Roman Catholic West that sought to differentiate themselves from the East by adopting this label (p. 33).

4 At one point, Machiavelli complains bitterly that "men are ever more taken with the things of the present than with those of the past" (ch. 24).

makes a prince so much esteemed as the undertaking of great enterprises and the setting a noble example in his own person" (ch. 21). Thus, Machiavelli urges the ambitious ruler to be "willing to follow the examples of those distinguished men who have redeemed their countries" (ch. 26). It stands to reason therefore that he would suggest studying a leader such as Clovis. Machiavelli himself claims that he would restrict himself to instances from Italy and recent instances (ch. 13), yet this does not prevent a shrewd leader from looking to another time and place for exemplars. Toward the end of *The Prince*, Machiavelli writes, "Amongst the well-organised and well-governed kingdoms of our time is that of France, which has a great many excellent institutions that secure the liberty and safety of the king" (ch. 19). Again, it stands to reason that many of the features that caused Machiavelli to fear France also drew his admiration.

Machiavelli devotes his little book to principalities, which is what Clovis obtained as his father's son and the elected chief of the warriors. Soon, however, Clovis burst the boundaries of his hereditary principality, which Machiavelli considered relatively easy to maintain (ch. 2). Clovis did that by appending nearby territories and gaining the loyalty of their fighting men, such that he was indeed creating a new principality, which Machiavelli considered much harder to obtain. Thus, Francia was to become a new principality comprised of the hereditary principality and the extensive appurtenances annexed to that estate (ch. 1). None of these territories had previously existed as free states, since they had been under Roman rule for centuries, making them relatively easier to obtain and certainly easier to maintain. Furthermore, Clovis obtained these territories mostly by his own military prowess, depending rarely on the arms of others (chaps. 3 & 6) – a fact that Machiavelli applauds.

Machiavelli notes that territory would be easier to obtain and maintain when you share the same language and something of the same basic culture (ch. 3). In this, Clovis had been fortunate to know and use Latin, which had been the *lingua franca* of Gaul. Also, he was baptized into the Roman Catholic faith, a religion widespread throughout Gaul despite the sweep of Arian immigrants. Machiavelli actually cites France as a region with shared manners and customs (ch. 3). Even so, Clovis was not too unlike the other barbarian tribes he would have encountered as opposition (see Geary, 1988, pp. 53f & 95f). Under these conditions, Machiavelli advises the victorious prince to extinguish the line of his predecessor (chs. 3 & 4; see also *The Discourses*, I, 9), so as to eradicate any hint of a revival of that dynasty, which is something that Clovis did routinely, with singular diligence. Machiavelli writes, "When the line of the [predecessor] is once extinguished, the inhabitants, being on the one hand accustomed to obey, and on the other having lost their ancient sovereign [i.e., Rome], can neither agree to create a new one from amongst themselves, nor do they know how to live in liberty; and thus they will be less prompt to take up arms, and the new prince will readily be able to gain their good will" (ch. 5). Another thing Machiavelli recommends is working with existing local officials, rather than simply relying on one's army as an occupation force (ch. 3). This Clovis did.

Some princes govern alone, regarding everyone else subject to a single author- ity; Machiavelli does not prefer that arrangement to a system of one prince with nobles (citing France, actually), with their intermediate rank (ch. 4). This arrange- ment requires a certain degree of dependence on these nobles. Yet Machiavelli is not describing a two-tiered system, for he regards the lower classes to be essential to a prince's long-term success. In this case, Machiavelli advises, the wise leader will immediately "strive to win the good will of the people . . . by taking them under his protection" (ch. 9). He will need their support, perhaps even against his own nobles sometime later. In other words, Machiavelli favors a *three-part structure*.

Machiavelli makes an interesting assertion in chapter 11 to the effect that ecclesiastical principalities "are the only ones that are secure and happy." This judgment bodes ill for every other type. Yet, in the specific instance of Clovis and Francia, one could reasonably ask to what extent it qualified as an ecclesiastical principality. Did the embrace of Catholicism and repeated acts of solicitousness by Clovis qualify Francia as such a regime? The church did not govern in its own name, of course, as it would in the Vatican; yet Machiavelli is not necessarily expecting that. He is still writing about princes whose authority comes under the aegis of the church, and this was true of Clovis: advised by bishops, person- ally and in council, coronated by a bishop, married to a saint, Clovis supported the church explicitly and refused to loot its property. He even erected a center of worship. Sebastian Scholz (2019) refers to "a highly autonomous and important Frankish church" that with time could criticize and coerce even the pope. This makes sense, inasmuch as it had grown independently and managed its own affairs for years, without any interference from Rome, thus unifying an entire nation when Italy itself was occupied by the Ostrogoths and then scattered into a variety of lesser city-states (see Haun, 2013, p. 30). Machiavelli obsequiously declines to analyze ecclesiastical regimes, writing that their existence is attributable to Divine Power, which is beyond his capacity to comprehend.

The power he did presume to comprehend was military. Machiavelli begins by observing, "The desire of conquest is certainly most natural and common amongst men" (ch. 3). Consequently, war is a condition of life and not to be avoided (ch. 3). In fact, writes Machiavelli, "when [princes] depend upon their own strength . . . then they rarely incur any danger" (ch. 6). In chapter 10, he argues that the best measure of a leader's success is whether princes "who, from an abundance of men and money, can put a well-appointed army into the field, and meet anyone in open battle that may attempt to attack them." He writes that this is how one should measure *all* principalities (making no exception here for ecclesiastical principalities). Not coincidentally, after his chapter on ecclesiasti- cal principalities, he asserts that the main foundations that *all* states must have are good laws and good armies. Then, he claims that there can be no good laws without good armies (ch. 12), and for that army to be most effective, the prince himself must assume command (ch. 12). In fact, Machiavelli gives as his historical example of a failure to command good armies the collapse of the Roman Empire, when Romans turned over the onus of combat to non-Romans and left it to peoples such as the Franks to secure the border (ch. 13). Small wonder, therefore, that these warlike peoples displaced the empire and created their own in its stead.[5]

In chapter 14, Machiavelli writes, "A prince, then, should have no other thought or object so much at heart, and make no other thing so much his especial study, as the art of war and the organization and discipline of his army; for that is the only art that is expected of him who commands." This admonition suits any description of Clovis I, elected as a war chief, successful in battle, and for many years apparently *laissez-faire* with regard to other aspects of the realm.[6]

Later in *The Prince*, Machiavelli warns the prospective prince about external and internal threats. For the former, he recommends good arms – the better to repulse attacks with, as we have just seen. Coincidentally, success against foreign foes by means of a powerful army also happens to reduce *internal* threats (ch. 19). The people admire and fear a leader successful against foreign enemies. Nevertheless, the goal is not simply to intimidate one's own subjects, even if the leader is not above relying on coercion. Intimidation is not exclusively what success in battle accomplishes. The prince should not gratuitously coerce his own people when he doesn't have to. Instead, his subjects will interpret his battlefield successes as evidence of his overall competence. He is keeping the peace, which everyone may enjoy, and this fact gains a prince favor. Machiavelli writes that "the people love quiet" (ch. 19). In addition, writes Machiavelli, battlefield exploits win respectful and satisfied admiration from the people (ch. 19).

As to individual traits, Machiavelli is careful to explain that a *reputation* for virtue is more important than actually possessing it. People judge by their eyes and can be fooled. On occasion, it is indeed best to fool them. Toward this end, religion can be used as a pretext (ch. 21). Also, Machiavelli notes that princes who rely on "plunder, pillage and exactions" can and should share the booty liberally (ch. 16) – a practice long settled by the Franks until Clovis excluded from the plunder that property which had belonged to the church. As to cruelty, which Machiavelli addresses in chapter 17, a prince can afford to risk a reputation for

---

5 In another passage, Machiavelli recommends that princes "should devolve all matters of responsibility upon others, and take upon themselves only those of grace" (ch. 73). He does not resolve this apparent contradiction in the pages of *The Prince*: do you command troops directly or let others lead? Nevertheless, it bears repeating that Clovis commanded his own army in the field, yet in other matters he appears to have delegated authority. And toward the end of his reign, he explicitly convened various experts to formulate what the prevailing laws and religion would look like in what would become known as Francia. In this, he resembles the leader Machiavelli writes about in another place, i.e., *The Discourses* (I, 9).

6 Fouracre (2022) calls it "light touch" government (p. 49). In a similar fashion, Yitzhak Hen (2022) explains that unlike the Roman practice, the Merovingian court was "less rigid and more adaptable" (p. 219).

cruelty. He writes that "a few displays of severity will really be more merciful than [allowing], by an excess of clemency, disorders to occur, which are apt to result in rapine and murder" (ch. 17). In this (utilitarian) way, the prince limits the injury to the individual victim and does not plunge the entire community into chaos. After all, in the next chapter of *The Prince,* Machiavelli admits that a leader's actions are judged by their results, regardless of any actual intent (ch. 18). This is especially so within the military, where a reputation for cruelty is, in his opinion, always necessary. The opening anecdote about the vase of Soissons exemplifies this tactic of a strategic use of cruelty.

In this section, I have posed the hypothesis that, whether he intended this or not, Machiavelli's "prince" resembles Clovis in many important respects. Scholars more familiar with Machiavelli's biography might be able to supply further evidence, one way or the other, about whether Machiavelli did indeed intend Clovis as an exemplar, but the similarities are striking.

A broader pattern of suffrage

In 1983, Michel Serres published the first of three books in a series about the founding of Rome. Bloomsbury Academic came out with a translation into English by Randolph Burks in 2015 titled *Rome: The First Book of Foundations.*

Serres first makes a comparison, as follows: just as the idea of "substance" preceded the study of physics, so also there is an idea that precedes the social sciences, of which leadership studies is a part. Substance is not any longer a scientific term; instead, it is a catchall for the stuff, the underlying reality that physics sets out to investigate. "What is this stuff? How does it come to be? What are its properties?" In the same manner, the social sciences set out to investigate something else, something Serres refers to as "suffrage." The term sounds peculiar to modern ears, but he explains that the term comes from the root for breaking apart and coming back together (1983/2015, p. 108). In politics, we use the term commonly to reflect the process by which a people come together to vote – that is, to elect representatives. Then the people disperse and go about their business. They gather to do one thing, then they scatter. For Serres, this pattern of collecting or gathering into some kind of unity, then breaking apart again into a multiplicity over and over, is the "stuff" that the social sciences such as leadership studies exist to explicate.

People meet, for example, in order to conduct trade. They assemble to enjoy performances and to worship. They organize themselves into large groups and small groups, into corporations, clubs, teams, juries, audiences, congregations, alliances, partnerships, communities, families, neighborhoods, nations, armies, cast and crew, parties, mobs, and conspiracies. But then they subdivide or disassemble or adjourn or melt away. What Serres is describing is a continuous, pulsating flux, at multiple levels, for multiple purposes and durations, the becoming of unities and then returning into multiplicities. Political science, economics, sociology, and presumably leadership studies concentrate on different aspects of the same never-ending dynamic.

Serres offers a colorful example that occurs in the course of a single evening (1983/2015, p. 111). Audience members arrive at the concert hall, chatting and chuckling, generating a familiar buzz. Just before the curtain rises, they all hush. They behave as one. They become an audience. The orchestra delivers its program which it had rehearsed for many hours, and the audience joins them in the shared experience. They are united by the music. At the conclusion of the performance, the unity of the audience continues more or less when they all applaud – not exactly in unison, but at the same moment in time and for the same reason – but then as that shared noise subsides, they break up into smaller groups and into couples, chatting again in private conversations which restore that original low-level din as everybody leaves the venue to go home. Noise (multiplicity) – silence – music (unity) – applause – noise (multiplicity). This is what Serres means by "suffrage": a process of breaking apart, as in fragments, and then coming together again. When a person is said to have been extended the right to suffrage, to have won suffrage, this means they are included in this rhythm. That is, when the people turn to select leaders, they get to be part of that; and then once that business has concluded, they are free to go live their separate, private lives.

From within this conceptual framework, a dynamic pattern by which individuals convene or swarm, then dismantle their collectivity, leadership represents a phase of unity, like music above the tumult, a temporary cessation of multiplicity, chaos, and noise. As scholars, we hope to understand these fluxions. And especially, we wish to know who in particular participates in these dynamics, and how they do it. One might argue that leadership periodically establishes a unity, redefining the boundaries and reacquainting everyone with a unifying purpose in light of changing conditions.

Most of the book by Serres is about the founding of Rome. Rome stands out as the historical exemplar. How did this city begin? We speak as though Rome has a foundation, a starting point, a font. We just want to know what it is and how it happened. Serres points out that there was always something *before* the object of our studies, chronologically, just as there is always something beneath the city walls – a foundation of sorts for the foundation. Every foundation is preceded by a multiplicity. Out of this multiplicity, a unity emerges; and before that multiplicity, a prior unity. According to legend, for example, Rome was preceded in time by Troy; its legends were believed to explain where the Romans came from. In space, it was preceded by the people of Alba; its city was razed, so that Rome was erected on the tombs of the vanquished. The creation of Rome is but an episode in a recurring pattern of turbulence, albeit a remarkable suspension of the broadest tumult. In fact, Serres argues that the very etymology of the terms "empire" and "imperial" means a unity comprised of multiplicities, which he calls "the unintegrable multiplicity" (1983/2015, p. 84) – a unity at a higher level of abstraction that in some way holds diverse forces together.

Toward the end of that magnificent unification we call the Roman Empire, everything reverted to multiplicity – multiple peoples, multiple religions, multiple powers – with all the accompanying noise. Clovis stepped in and brought into existence another unity, a subsequent unity, founding a new regime.

Lest we misunderstand, Serres is not comfortable describing a linear progression from Troy to Rome across time or from Alba to Rome as layers in the dirt. Time is not in that sense linear. It is not, as he says, a continuum. From our vantage point, looking backwards, we tend to conceive it that way, but the reality is far more bewildering. There is no single line from point A to point B. There are multiple crisscrossing lines, coming and going, up one side and down the other, i.e., lines that appear to have converged on the founding of Rome. Nevertheless, at the same time, other things were certainly going on, such as commerce between Greeks, conquest atop the central-Asian steppe, worship among the wood-hidden Celts. And in fact, as Serres explains in several ways, the very founding itself was a massive disaggregation of powers and peoples, thronging and scattering, because any unity exacts a price or penalty. Romulus killed his twin. Romulus in his turn was blasted apart by the gods. Somebody has to die for another to be born. And in the transformation that results, many elements mingling in the cluster are to be sacrificed. Some people must perish. Some religions must pass away. Some practices must discontinue. As Serres puts it, "Foundation happens when multiplicity becomes unity. The multiple hardens around the unity of the corpse" (1983/2015, p. 194).

As we saw in this chapter, the past that confronts us in the twenty-first century is itself a multiplicity, tattered and interwoven, requiring powers of interpretation (Serres, 1983/2015, p. 13).[7] Ordinarily, any foundation of one thing means the demise or eradication of something else – or, more accurately, a unification where multiplicity had previously prevailed. *Something* always preceded a founding (Serres, 1983/2015, p. 24). What it was exactly will be hard for us to discern because a multiplicity is a stratum of noise, confusion, and turbulence. Combing through the records, the archaeological evidence, the various subsequent histories written in the interim – history itself is a great deal of noise (Serres, 1983/2015, p. 26). No account of the past, no matter how brilliant or exhaustive, can uncover the entirety of what transpired. Choices in interpretation have to be made in the telling of that story. And then the story unfolds according to a particular logic that by necessity omits so much else (Serres, 1983/2015, p. 61).

Having said this, however, Serres goes on to contend that the unifying figure who stands at the foundation of a regime (in this case, Clovis) represents a unity of disparate things or, as he puts it, "the intersection of the opposing sets"

---

7 Serres goes so far as to claim that history is comprised of myth, yet it hides that fact by pretending to be objective and true (1983/2015, p. 189).

(1983/2015, p. 199). He is the intersection of enemies, the intersection of functions, the intersection of unrelated groups. He stands at the confluence, a singular point or "phase transition" (p. 201), permitting everybody to forget the multiplicity and imagine everything now reconciled anew. From a distance, of course, the characters come and go, leaders emerge and pass away, while that energy cloud of suffrage pulsates repeatedly – again, in a pattern of coming together and diffusing (p. 216). Clovis would be as a knot of many threads. His success, though, can be said to have derived from his capacity to tolerate, if not exploit, the multiplicities, the liminal turbulence, the many identities and interests and hatreds that reasserted themselves after centuries of Roman dominance (p. 229).

The base multiplicity

The period of time immediately preceding the rise of Clovis qualifies as liminal, on a massive scale. One immense and aging empire (Roman) was on the wane, and an existential threat from the east (Hun) forced multiple warring tribes (barbarians) to flee westward into the lands of that tottering regime, which included the territory of Gaul. Geary (1988) adds that, so far as historians can tell, the situation throughout the land we now refer to as Germany was one of "disequilibrium and stress" due to various shifts, migrations, and conquests (p. 60). Pagan religions (e.g., Celtic and Roman) were giving way to two closely related monotheistic faiths (orthodox Christianity and Arianism) at roughly the same time that Christianity found itself divided further geographically into an eastern and western expression, centered in Constantinople and Rome, respectively. The migrating peoples known as barbarians were themselves divided into tribes (e.g., Burgundian and Goth); furthermore, the one tribe of specific interest to us at this time was itself only loosely affiliated (Franks). Multiple religions, cultures, political systems, and legal systems were represented in the contested territory of Gaul.

The Franks themselves straddled three cultures: the barbarian, the Roman, and the Roman Catholic. Every year, the warriors of that modest tribe decided where to campaign that season, so that there was a degree of uncertainty about long-term policy. Also, on the occasion of a vacancy, they elected a war leader as chief.[8] That war leader's authority was considerably constrained by tradition to matters of warfare and the will of his assembled soldiers. Their entire economy tended to rest on plunder, which they shared among themselves, and on tribute; it was a paradoxical arrangement inasmuch as the empire where they now found themselves had tended to rely on agriculture and trade, such that without those activities, there would have been very little in the vicinity to plunder. (Unable to feed themselves by scavenging, the Visigoths had just kept migrating westward.)

8 Joseph Canning (1996) points out that even prior to the emergence of Clovis, rulership in the Roman polity was ambiguously dependent on both divine sanction and popular support, so that leaders had to pay attention to both sources of authority (pp. 9 & 19).

Despite the fact that the Franks had been known at one time as a sea-going people, their forays into Gaul tended to make them dependent on the land. Consequently, as the Franks gradually assumed a greater role in the Roman system prevailing at the time in Gaul, they were expected not to plunder the lands over which they had been ceded control. Yet Franks were not interested much in farming or commerce. In addition, Frankish law was quite different from Roman law, let alone the incipient church law, so there was some understandable confusion as to jurisdiction and the administration of justice. This had yet to be worked out (see Rio, 2022, ch. 23).

A wise leader under these bewildering conditions would have to be adaptable.

While the barbarians competed for supremacy across the entire continent and engaged in geopolitics at the highest level, at the local level, tension existed between a landed gentry firmly ensconced in a rural context with their seasonal routines and the bishoprics presiding over increasingly significant urban centers, where proximity and exchange generated novelty and connected cities across Christendom laterally. As de Landa (2000) describes this tension, Gaul consisted of (a) consolidated centers of local authority, preserving traditions and securing an identity as they radiated control outward in a concentric pattern, and (b) meshworks where different kinds of people with different traditions and interests negotiated a way to live together for their mutual benefit, in more of a diffuse network across boundaries. One sees these meshworks arise in port cities, on border towns, and during festivals that attracted people from far away. De Landa neglected to write about a third type of community that was to acquire considerable importance in the Middle Ages, namely, the monastery, which in a manner of speaking became isolated, set apart from the rest of the world by design, with more of an inward focus (see generally Wood, 1994, ch. 11; Brown, 1971). As king, Clovis would have to manage very different *kinds* of communities.

So many heterogeneous factors shaped the political landscape – many of which were entirely new – that it would have been difficult to know how to lead one's people effectively. The clear hierarchies of Rome were collapsing. The hierarchy of the church was in its early stages, retarded in its development by the vacancy at Rome. Thus, the church was more of what we might call a polycentric agglomeration, with local hierarchies. The loosely democratic structure of the barbarian tribes was ill-suited for governing this elaborate expanse of Gaul in any sustainable manner. Leadership training as it existed at the time consisted of formal education, for many, transitioning away from classical education in the Roman ethos and toward religious schooling, with its catechisms – neither of which were readily available nor genuinely valued by the Franks, who preferred the rude apprenticeship of warfare. It was certainly unclear which type of education would prepare prospective leaders (see, e.g., Brown, 1971, p. 32).

There were multiple, interlocking systems in various stages of development that made people vulnerable. Scholars of this period have mentioned repeatedly that one of the key variables in the absence of a unifying, mature social system (such as the Roman Empire had been and feudalism would become) was leadership. Some leaders were more effective in this bewildering and shifting context than others. Frequently, historians will fix on a specific person as singular. That is, they will focus their research on the outsized social agents who appeared to make a difference. Soon enough, the entire system would solidify, formalizing and giving a degree of predictability and stability to Europe, in a process familiar to readers of Max Weber. But the era of Clovis more narrowly was, in the most radical sense, liquid (Bauman, 2007). Because of this, his personal initiative was critical to the establishment of a durable regime. His leadership stands out as dominant, adaptable, and far-sighted, as evidenced by the growth and consolidation of the kingdom in his lifetime, as well as by its extraordinary longevity. In a time without clear lines of authority, leadership fosters the emergence of a new order.

The evidence of a new order that became France is unquestioned. Beginning with Charlemagne, France dominated Christianized Europe. Working backwards, by negative inference, we probably ought to look for the leader who made this all possible. That is one reason why it pays to consider Clovis – especially because so many prospective leaders rose in that epoch. Some such as Attila the Hun and Geiseric the Vandal were outsiders pursuing their own agenda; some such as Flavius Constantius and Flavius Aetius were the consummate insiders who tried to restore the grandeur that was Rome. Some such as Theodoric II the Amal and Alaric II the Visigoth played a role similar to the one adopted by Clovis, emerging from among the barbarians and working on behalf of their tribe, but also hoping to secure a place within the Roman Empire. Because so many leaders come and go, enjoying different degrees of success, that is why I do not take the position that, except for Clovis, there was no leadership whatsoever. There was actually plenty – perhaps too many leaders to accommodate them all (see Heather, 2006, p. 384). However, the proof of the leadership of Clovis is, as they say, in the pudding. The study of other leaders from that era – many of whom were admirable and successful – demonstrates the extent to which they were less successful than Clovis. In a turbulent era with multiple power centers and ambitious characters coming to the fore, Clovis did something remarkable and enduring.

Michel Serres (1995/2017) has described the rhythms of our inquiry. This book began telling a simple, linear story: A → B → C. In fact, although we began by asking whether it was a story about the end of antiquity or the beginning of the Middle Ages, we realized that it covers a period of transition from one to the other. Where exactly does our narrative begin and end? Nevertheless, we also saw that different historians offer different "linear" versions of events, hoping to replace prior versions with one of their own, so that we are confronted with multiple versions of A → B → C. Embedded in these versions are multiple, intersecting histories about the disintegration of the Roman Empire, the migration of entire peoples westward, and the entrenchment of the Roman Catholic Church, all taking place at multiple social layers. For some, it was a time of ascendancy and progress; for others, a time of deterioration and ruin; for yet others, just a continuation of life at the plow, tending the hearth or retrieving firewood. Each pattern can be true for the exact same time period.

At every founding, though, a people must go through three distinct phases:

(a) a **cleansing**, seeking purification, clarity, meaning (provided by the church);

(b) a **defending**, setting boundaries and securing them against incursions (provided by Clovis and the Franks); and

(c) a **cultivating**, putting the territory to work, bending to the productive possibilities of an enclosed space (provided by the landowners and their laborers).

As Heather points out, three things had to happen, and Clovis oversaw them all: "Legitimate authority had to be restored; the number of players needing to be conciliated by any incoming regime had to be reduced; and the Empire's revenues had to rise" (2006, p. 392).

References

Ando, C. (2008, Spring). "Decline, fall, and transformation." *Journal of Late Antiquity*. *1*(1): 31–60.

Bauman, Z. (2007). *Liquid times: Living in an age of uncertainty*. Polity.

Braudel, F. (1980). *On history* (S. Matthews, trans.). University of Chicago Press.

Brown, P. (1971). *The world of Late Antiquity, AD 150–750*. Thames & Hudson, Ltd.

Canning, J. (1996). *A history of medieval political thought, 300–1450*. Routledge.

de Landa, M. (2000). *A thousand years of nonlinear history*. Swerve Books.

de Montaigne, M. (1887). *Essays of Michel de Montaigne* (C. Cotton, trans.). Project Gutenberg.

Foucault, M. (1997). *"Society must be defended": Lectures at the College de France, 1975–76* (D. Macey, trans.). Picador.

Fouracre, P. (2022). "From Gaul to Francia: The impact of the Merovingians." In Effros, B. & Moreira, I. (eds.). *The Oxford handbook of the Merovingian world* (ch. 2). Oxford University Press.

Geary, P. (1988). *Before France and Germany: The creation and transformation of the Merovingian world*. Oxford University Press.

Halsall, G. (2014). "Two worlds become one: A 'counter-intuitive' view of the Roman Empire and 'Germanic' migration." *German History*. *32*(4): 515–532.

Harter, N. (2020). *Leadership across boundaries: A passage to Aporia*. Routledge.

Haun, J. (2013, May). "A new system of power: The Franks and the Catholic church in post-Roman Gaul." (Doctoral dissertation. University of Texas at Arlington).

Heather, P. (2006). *The fall of the Roman Empire: A new history of Rome and the Barbarians*. Oxford University Press.

Hen, Y. (2022). "The Merovingian polity: A network of courts and courtiers." In Effros, B. & Moreira, I. (eds.). *The Oxford handbook of the Merovingian world* (ch. 10). Oxford University Press.

Machiavelli, N. (1997). *The prince* (C.E. Detmold, trans.). Wordsworth Classics of World Literature.

Pelikan, J. (1987). *The excellent empire: The fall of Rome and the triumph of the church*. Harper & Row.

Rio, A. (2022). "Merovingian legal cultures." In Effros, B. & Moreira, I. (eds.). *The Oxford handbook of the Merovingian world* (ch. 23). Oxford University Press.

Scholz, S. (2019). "The papacy and the Frankish bishops in the sixth century." In Esders, S., Fox, Y., Hen, Y. & Sarti, L. (eds.). *East and West in the Early Middle Ages: The Merovingian kingdoms in Mediterranean perspective* (ch. 8). Cambridge University Press.

Serres, M. (1995/2017). *Geometry: The third book of foundations* (R. Burks, trans.). Bloomsbury Academic.

Serres, M. (1983/2015). *Rome: The first book of foundations* (R. Burks, trans.). Bloomsbury Academic.

Wilson, S. (2016). *Thinking differently about leadership: A critical history of leadership studies*. Edward Elgar.

Wood, I. (2017). *The transformation of the Roman west*. Arc Humanities Press.

Wood, I. (2013). *The modern origins of the early Middle Ages*. Oxford University Press.

Wood, I. (1994). *The Merovingian kingdoms, 450–751*. Longman.

5

POSSIBLE IMPLICATIONS FOR THE TWENTY-FIRST CENTURY

Introduction to the chapter

Historians disagree about whether their findings about the past predict the future. The past may have shaped the present, but it is still within our power in the present to choose where we will go next. At the same time, similar experiences from the past could easily unfold the same way in the present. At the moment of choosing, to what extent does society look to the past for guidance, whether to affirm something praiseworthy or to avoid anything blameworthy?

Concretely, in a liminal era, we can expect to witness the emergence of leadership as a determinative factor. Given the confusion, very little else explains the process by which new systems formalized and consolidated to endure for centuries. Nevertheless, as the example of Clovis illustrates, leaders emerged from every level of society – levels oftentimes working together, but occasionally working at cross-purposes, until a rough sense of order took hold in Francia. No single social actor in isolation designed that order. In fact, Clovis quite openly yielded to the authority of experts on agriculture, religion, and the law. He provided the holding environment within which this novel system could be nurtured. In an era of uncertainty, the leader set boundaries and held the realm secure, which was itself a significant contribution, but then he put in place a framework that did not require him to design the rest. Even so, we wouldn't want to overstate the unity of France in the time of Clovis; consolidation did not really take place until the reign of Charlemagne more than two hundred years later.[1]

---

1 Furthermore, the specific contours of the realm changed in many respects down through the ages. Dynasties rose and fell. Boundaries shifted. Regions contended, one with another. Fortunes were made and squandered. Paul Fouracre notes recently that Francia would survive, never being conquered, evolving for fifteen hundred years in a recognizable form (2020a, 2020b, pp. 37 & 60).

DOI: 10.4324/9781003297802-5

Ralph Mathisen writes, "The marquee political event of antiquity that has the greatest resonance in the modern day is almost certainly the decline and fall of the western Roman Empire in the fifth century" (2019, p. 137). Scholars continue to quarrel over what exactly happened then, let alone what it might mean for us today. Was it all a dramatic clash between Romans on the one side and barbarians on the other? Or was it a relatively peaceful, slow-motion merger of the two peoples? Or (for that matter) is it in truth a misnomer to think in these bilateral terms, i.e., Romans and barbarians? The Franks at the time of Clovis were, in Mathisen's words, "an integral part of the Roman world [who] looked and behaved little differently from frontier Romans" (2019, p. 139). By then, the term "Roman" was more of an umbrella term for the lot of them, including the Franks (see, e.g., Bileta, 2016, p. 24).

Nevertheless, Clovis represents a period of change, a transition point, no matter how gradual or confused. Not every era begins with a singular event, such as the French Revolution, and it is reasonable to assume that people at that time could not see events the way that we do now, on the tides of history. If anything, the career of Clovis suggests that the novelist Leo Tolstoy was wrong: kings are not necessarily the slaves of history. Sometimes, they are history itself.

In the bewildering conditions of a liminal state, one's attention is readily drawn to two things: that which persists in the time of confusion and that which describes an arc of discernible movement. Clovis is primarily the latter. What he made possible is the former. Everything else requires a magnifying glass and patience in order to notice, identify, and describe. History most certainly comprises many things, a bewildering confluence of interlocking narratives. Yet the predominating interest of newcomers and laymen lies in the origins of order and in leadership, for liminality is, as Bjørn Thomassen puts it, "an age of uncertainty, when possibilities lay open; a period when individuals were put to the test and new leadership figures arose" (2015, p. 51; see also p. 52f).[2]

The study of history gives to those of us in the present a sense of perspective. Not only will it tell us how we got here, but in some instances, it might give us advice on where to turn next. Historical evidence increases in value as we become disoriented in our own times, uncertain where we are and where we should go. Happily, historical evidence is the best, most reliable evidence that we have about how the social world works – better than social theory itself or controlled experiments, because history is what actually happened. By the same token, however, no two episodes are completely identical. There will be significant differences to take into consideration when trying to learn from the past. We cannot simply import lessons from another time and place, expecting them to work again now, without some adaptation. In short, what we must ask is some

---

2 Mark Allen Peterson (2015) points out that large-scale liminality can be defined by the absence of a predetermined leader (p. 176), when nobody is running the show.

version of the following question: "What is there in barbarism that we can make use of" (Foucault, 1997, p. 197)?

Plainly, no two historical epochs are identical. I am reluctant to go so far as to hold that history conforms to a pattern, such that certain stages in a process will resemble certain other epochs because they purportedly fall into the same niche in a recurring pattern: A then B then C then back to A, and so on. Others have made the argument – others such as Vico, Hegel, Marx, and Comte, to name a few – though I am not required in these pages to accept what they had to say. What I will accept is the notion of "periodicity," by which one can organize the past into phases or stages (Thomassen, 2015, p. 51f; see Nelson, 2020, p. 63). Even so, there are bound to be resemblances, similarities, between one epoch and another – at least with regard to isolated features they have in common. One thinks, for example, of a postwar or post-conflict detumescence. Such similarity can be instructive.[3]

I would argue instead that, rather than recurring patterns that obey some sort of historical law, there will be rough, approximate resemblances *among periods of transition*, which are also known as "disruptions" and "liminality." These phases-between-phases will exhibit a degree of uncertainty, confusion, upheaval in unexpected ways – conflict and complexity as the previous epoch falls apart and the next epoch struggles among rivals to take its place. As Horvath, Szakolczai, and Marangudakis (2020) explain:

> In its most general sense, a liminal situation is a temporary moment of transition in between two stable states, whether in the life course of an individual, or the conditions of a community . . . a void situation where unexpected and even threatening things can happen.
>
> *(p. 4)*

Agnes Horvath (2020) even calls them "world-historical turning points" (p. 16).

Such periods of turbulence will resemble one another, at least to that extent. It may be the case that one's liminal condition is like other liminal epochs; and if so, then perhaps we can learn something from the past about how folks managed to make their way through. At the very least, we might learn what made matters *worse*. Frequently (though not always), the way forward out of one's shared liminal condition will entail this thing we call leadership.

My argument looks like this.

Step one.   You and I live in liminal times.
Step two.   Humanity has passed through liminal times before.

---

3 Paul Fouracre (2022) points out that, coincidentally, as a leader Clovis faced two crises that confront the world again at the time I am writing this book: climate change and a pandemic (p. 39).

Step three.   In our consideration of liminality now, we might learn something from previous episodes.

Step four.   One mechanism for surviving liminal times has been leadership.

Any fine-grained analysis of the past will find multiple periods of liminality. Such a period might be brief, i.e., nearly imperceptible, or merely amusing. It might affect only one sector of society or an isolated geographic region. Individual social actors pass through stages of liminality throughout their lives. There is plenty of evidence of these experiences, at every magnitude. Bjørn Thomassen (2015) even created a typology along three dimensions, as follows:

(a) a dimension of **magnitude**, ranging from the individual experience (micro) to the upheaval of entire societies (macro);

(b) a dimension of **duration**, ranging from a momentary experience to decades and generations of upheaval; and

(c) a dimension of **space**, from the simple village threshold or gate to entire geographic regions.

(p. 48f)

I am interested here in periods that are large in scale and significance, such as epidemics, famine, mass migrations, war, revolutions, and the rise of popular new religions. Even though each of these phenomena is a distinct type of challenge (a famine is not a war) and each discrete instance of each type of challenge is unique (among wars, the War of the Roses is not the Boer War), I am pondering the possibility that all of them have liminality itself in common. And in my case, I am pondering an enduring societal upheaval throughout an entire region.

More narrowly, I intended to concentrate on the leadership of a solitary person. For antiquity, that person was Clovis I, king of the Franks (c. 466–511 CE). For McCarthyism in a following section, it is Edward R. Murrow, a pioneer of broadcast journalism (1908–1965). To be sure, many thousands of social actors shaped their times and not just one. Yet these two historical figures (Clovis and Murrow) appear in retrospect to have had a disproportionate impact. Certainly, when they were alive, they were acknowledged to be men of consequence. It appears to be the judgment of history as well that they were quite as consequential as they had seemed, if not more so. Once again, however, I must acknowledge that these two men were not exactly alike; their leadership was different in response to different times. I do not expect to show that the way forward from liminality is only one type of leadership. Leaders' styles can be different from one another and still help me make the case that – however it is practiced – leadership itself was (and can be) consequential.[4]

---

4 I anticipate an objection. It may be the case that I am indulging in a tautology, because of course history will record that the way forward through liminality was leadership, because human agency

Learning from liminality

Liminality can prove to be a useful topic in the social sciences, even a "master concept" (Thomassen, 2015, p. 39). The editors of a volume on varieties of liminality (a book titled *Breaking Boundaries*) posit that "liminal conditions of irrationality are situations to be studied in their own right" (Horvath et al., 2015, p. 2). They can be said to possess "logics of their own" (p. 2). Accordingly, these scholars assembled a number of studies for the express purpose of "undertak[ing] comparisons across historical periods" (2015, p. 3) – much as I have done.

These editors define the term "liminality" to depict "in-between situations and conditions characterized by dislocation of established structures, the reversal of hierarchies, and uncertainty about the continuity of tradition and future outcomes" (2015, p. 2). Later, they refer to "outbreaks of liminal conditions in a large-scale setting entailing genuine collapse of order and loss of stable reference points" (2015, p. 6). At such times, we are told, there is no law (Szakolczai, 2015, p. 18). Often, students of history treat these episodes as disturbances that suggest something bad is going on. To be sure, that is often the case: something bad probably is going on, certainly from the point of view of guardians of the old order. Nevertheless, students also overlook the extent to which these episodes are also generative, creating a new order. They entail an identity change (Horvath, 2015, p. 89), but an identity change within some degree of continuity. Michel Dobry calls this his "theory of fluid conjunctures" (2015, p. 93). The flow of events continues, even though it brings about something new. Bernhard Giesen calls liminality indispensable to order (2015, p. 62). The problem is that people cannot ignore or classify these episodes neatly (2015, p. 64). What to do?

The tendency of scholars to portray society as binary – that is, as one thing or the other, or as two things in contrast with one another – overlooks the space between the two orienting poles of any schema (Giesen, 2015, p. 62). It can be tempting to begin with some kind of stark duality and then to plot the overcoming of the duality in a kind of resolution. According to Agnes Horvath, this temptation can lead to wishful thinking (2015, p. 74). Worse, in her opinion, people can just deny the essence of that which sets the two sides apart. The entire

---

is what we mean by leadership. Whenever we attribute change to anybody, that person was the leader; if it were not Clovis or Murrow, it would have been somebody else. Historians have often tended to go in search of leaders as one way to explain what happened (see, e.g., Carlyle, 1902). Perhaps the more interesting case would be the liminal epoch during which no leadership arose. Is that even possible? If not, then I wouldn't be saying anything new. I have Camil Francisc Roman (2015) to thank for portraying such an episode as occurring during the tumult following the French Revolution, when the authorities executed the last king as the unifying symbol of the nation (in 1793) while hoping to establish "the people" as the leader. It wasn't until 1799 when Napoleon Bonaparte finally emerged as the embodied leader of the French nation. In the interim was the so-called Reign of Terror (see Potter, 2021, ch. 4). In *The Red Wheel*, Alexander Solzhenitsyn offers a similar illustration from the Russian Revolution before Vladimir Lenin and the Bolshevists stepped in to impose order (1984–1991; see also Potter, 2021, ch. 5).

dichotomy is judged by constructivists, for example, to exist in the imagination. It is not real in any other sense. In this way, they dissolve the apparent tension. I am hoping to avoid that tactic here.

To be thorough, we will have to acknowledge that, during liminal epochs, there will continue to be a lot that carries on as normal, even routine. One is not required to think that everything abruptly changes all at the same time (Thomassen, 2015, p. 50). The period is both/and, with elements left over from the previous epoch and new elements that will solidify into a fresh configuration sometime later. And the period of Clovis is paradigmatic of this type of historical epoch. Clifford Ando writes, "I take it as axiomatic that the structures of Roman government in the west collapsed, and that the invasions that impelled the events embraced in that statement were traumatic" (2008, p. 40; see Ward-Perkins, 2005).

As I have been saying in different ways, the collapse of the Roman Empire was paradigmatically liminal.

In 2015, Michel Dobry questioned the value of the idea that liminal phases have an identity of their own. In retrospect, of course, we refer to a specific revolution or plague or mass migration as a way to categorize the outcome and then compare it to other instances, as though two historical crises with an equivalent outcome are comparable. In that way, a social scientist might presume to analyze revolutions (for example) in the abstract – including the *American* Revolution, the *French* Revolution, the *Russian* Revolution, and so on – identifying their shared etiology and characteristics. "This is what it means to undergo a revolution." Dobry argues instead that not only does this tactic tend to omit details that make each instance unique (e.g., the American Revolution and the French Revolution were not alike in significant ways), it also obscures the conditions that prevailed while it was happening. I think that this second observation deserves a closer look.

Social actors in the midst of a revolution are not always aware what is going on or where things are headed.

(a) Some of the people caught up in what we call a revolution are totally oblivious; it apparently makes no difference to them. I think, for example, of children or mental patients or solitary holy men living in a cave.

(b) Other people living in that time and place might be aware that something is going on, but they are largely unaffected. They still get up every day to milk the cows.

(c) By way of contrast, some among these people, such as Bolshevists, might agree on what they are trying to bring about, but they are a minority in the population, not always in full agreement among themselves, and totally incapable of predicting the actual flow of events, i.e., the unintended consequences, once they will have jumped into the situation. And chances are there would be other small groups, similarly motivated, such as Mensheviks, who also try to steer events toward a competing vision of a better world. Such episodes likely depict a struggle among rivals – rival ethnic groups, rival religions, rival ideologies, and so forth. There are other categories, also.

(d) Many people will experience the disruption as a threat to the status quo, perhaps motivating them to resist for the sake of preserving what they know and value. They may not know where things are going, but they probably won't like it, so they stand in opposition to the calls for change.

(e) Many others – possibly most – will simply flounder in anxiety, without knowing what any of it means because they are without the familiar points of reference they had come to trust. They directly experience the upheaval as such. The salient fact for them is that they are unable to ascribe any meaning to current events.[5]

Dobry explains that, in periods of relative stability, modern society structures itself according to discernible sectors such as commerce, religion, law, politics, and education. Each sector operates according to internal norms, governed by distinct elites. Nevertheless, part of the stability can be ascribed to the extent to which these elites reinforce one another. Businessmen use the court system and comply with legislation. Congressmen give tax advantages to businessmen. The media pay attention to the elite. And education prepares students to defer to existing elites and ultimately join them. There are, in short, interlocking and mutually reinforcing elites.[6] Nevertheless, despite this interwoven fabric, each sector has its unique traditions, its standards, its jargon, its ritual process. When these sectors collapse, when politics overruns them all, removing their distinctive character and throwing all of society into confusion, where then will people look for guidance? What norms will still matter? What game will everybody be trying to play once the game no longer exists? Dobry refers to these episodes using the ungainly term "desectorization." The constellation of social cues by which people orient themselves has vanished or shifted significantly – not here or there, incrementally, but altogether. He writes that "sector-specific social logics cease to function" (2015, p. 102). And once they go, representations of the old order become useless – or worse, targets of reprisal. People start concluding that now there is no justice, there is no law, there is no god.

How then do social actors orient themselves once the familiar constellations cannot be trusted? How do they "play" after the game has collapsed? People still have to make decisions. Do they go to work tomorrow? Do they flee the country? Do they buy shotguns and stock up on canned food? What folks likely want, says Dobry, whether they know it consciously or not, is a focal point, a symbol, a rallying center, such as a political party or a family or a figurehead. Or they run

---

5 The late work of Eric Voegelin pertains to this admixture of characters (1987, p. 25), including guardians of the status quo, adherents of rival movements, skeptics, and the indifferent.
6 Regarding the Frankish kingdom, see, e.g., Haun, 2013, p. 4.

to their churches to pray. They need a fixity, a sure thing. They need something to rely on.[7]

David Potter, writing in 2021, reduces episodes of disruption to a kind of rough formula. It begins with the collapse of the prevailing order, he writes; that is to say, the familiar structures and verities no longer seem to apply (pp. 34, 81, 138, & 273). In such a predicament, someone leading a small group of dedicated followers emerges to champion an alternative set of ideas. The ideas already existed somewhere, propagated by thought leaders such as Martin Luther or Karl Marx (Potter, 2021, p. 10); but now in the midst of uncertainty, a charismatic figure such as Vladimir Lenin picks up these ideas and presumes to apply them to the circumstances – usually making critical adaptations to reality, so that these ideas are no longer merely theoretical. Thus, this activist cadre needs an intellectual of some sort to apply the new ideas to the task of governing (p. 81). The intellectual might be the charismatic leader himself, as Lenin was, but it is not necessary. In Czechoslovakia, for instance, the first president after the fall of the Berlin Wall was Václav Havel, but his intellectual forebearer was a retiring philosopher by the name of Jan Patočka. In any case, the disruption requires both an ideology (to use Potter's term) and power (p. 137). Ideas and power are yoked together. To be sure, the originating ideas could become distorted as a result of this process, such that Christianity (to use one of Potter's examples) looks very different once Constantine makes it the imperial religion (p. 141). There is no necessary correlation between the originating ideas and their embodiment in reality. In fact, the same ideas can yield very different results in different contexts. Nevertheless, a crisis creates an opening for new ideas to emerge. Sometimes, these new ideas help to reinforce the existing system, reinvigorating it (as Constantine reinforced the Roman Empire and kept it going), and sometimes they call for replacing the existing system (as Lenin helped to replace Tsarism) (p. 285). It would be a mistake, however, to presuppose that these charismatic leaders and their entourages were ever true believers in the new ideas. Oftentimes, yes, they were authentic. We have no reason to doubt Lenin's zeal. Potter notes, however, the following: "Disruptions first and foremost serve the ends of the disrupters" (p. 286). Under Potter's formula, the collapse of the Western empire made it possible for Germanic forces represented by Clovis and his retinue to insinuate themselves, ostensibly under the guise of *preserving* the empire, yet on behalf of some combination of barbarian values and the Roman Catholic religion.

Going back to Dobry, it was at this moment in the argument that the author makes a strange and intriguing suggestion. People want to find a focal point during phases of liminality, as was stated previously. Dobry argues that this focal point

---

7 Previously, we had reason to question this framework in which crisis somehow causes the rise of charismatic leadership.

can be something or someone to hate, to despise, to draw away the unharnessed energy and send it toward a concrete nemesis, an object to blame, a scapegoat, perhaps, or a villain (see also Girard, 1989). The author Roman (2015) refers to this as the "anti-symbol" (p. 154). In times of structural uncertainty, writes Dobry, people search for something to latch onto, to give them a sense of what to do, whether that means (a) following a leader who seems to know a way forward (something positive, a symbol) or (b) marching with torches and pitchforks toward the author of their frustrations (something negative, an anti-symbol).[8]

It has been my contention that Clovis served as that positive symbol, a reliable point of reference, for the many in Francia who experienced one of the most consequential periods of liminality ever recorded in Europe. The people longed for some kind of stabilizing presence, a source of unity, and (true to the times) they looked upward, vertically, for an authority that transcended the ordinary world. They wanted someone extraordinary to fill the apparent power vacuum. Borrowing the categories of Max Weber, they sought charisma in the absence of reassuring traditions. Since that time, however, in a modern democracy, the people are expected to look elsewhere, horizontally, at one another, in what Harold Wydra calls radical indeterminacy and permanent dialogue, accepting that the power vacuum will *never* be filled. Instead, he argues, it must be renegotiated every election cycle. In a state or condition of liminality in a democracy, the quest for order accepts a degree of ineradicable uncertainty. It is, to borrow a phrase from Jacques Derrida, a structure without a center (1978, p. 278f).

To be sure, many today will abandon this horizontal image of authority and instead resort to the vertical again, hoping to identify the proverbial Man on a White Horse, a hero to rescue us from ourselves, a savior (see Potter, 2021, p. 27). In other words, they will look for a positive symbol. In contrast, many will turn against a common enemy and derive a sense of unity from identifying a scapegoat. In other words, they will latch onto an anti-symbol. In fact, if someone (a demagogue) emerges to lead us against that scapegoat, so much the better. That would appear to be the best of all possible worlds – except that it isn't. What I have been describing here is a recipe for fascism. In order to avert fascism – and this is an important insight – democracy struggles to *retain the liminality* and keep the seat of power empty, deriving its sense of order from something else, something we are meant to share, like a shared heritage or a shared founding or a shared constitution.

Let us consider, for example, the historical period immediately following World War II from the point of view of a victorious American populace, flush with success. A fraught alliance with the Soviet Union against the Axis powers had left Europe divided into spheres of influence – one of them dedicated to capitalism and liberal democracy (euphemistically known as the West) and one

---

8 He writes this, I hasten to mention, before Donald Trump became president of the United States.

of them dedicated to communism and global revolution. These two vast powers and their ideologies began a new struggle known as the Cold War, in which each side perceived the other as an existential threat, certainly as more than a mere competitor or adversary. Because a direct assault by either one of them could have launched a nuclear horror, each of them engaged in practices meant to supplant the other, primarily by means of tactics such as propaganda, espionage, and the sponsoring of surrogates in countries such as Korea and Vietnam.

The United States, a nation unfamiliar with the burdens of empire and without the orienting structure of a world war, was undergoing its own liminal period, not only in international relations and the military draw-down, reabsorbing hundreds of thousands of soldiers and sailors, but also economically and culturally. The populace was trying to make sense of myriad new inventions. Many of them, such as radar, promised civilian advantages; but one of them certainly, the atom bomb – a weapon beyond conceiving – threatened annihilation. And their mortal enemies were acquiring the technology to use the same weapons in response (or even perhaps preemptively).

Into this liminal phase stepped a political actor promising to thwart the enemy by revealing who in their midst was secretly working for the enemy. Joseph McCarthy made it his mission to expose the traitors, spies, and fellow travelers who wished America harm. He was not alone, of course, as many others took up the challenge of rooting out disloyalty – public figures including J. Edgar Hoover, Richard M. Nixon, and Robert Kennedy, to name a few. Media outlets (perhaps most notably the Hearst conglomerate) feverishly tracked the exploits of so-called red baiters, publicized widely in dramatic court cases and congressional hearings. Nevertheless, McCarthy was such a flamboyant and self-aggrandizing character central to the effort that the era has been named for him. Here was a self-appointed guardian (positive symbol) dedicated to eradicating a hidden menace (anti-symbol), thereby making sense of America's postwar condition. His exertions were a response to a pervading sense of vulnerability in the nation that emerged out of world war as ostensibly the most powerful and successful on the world stage.

Edward R. Murrow and the spirit of McCarthyism

The modern world has included experiments in self-governance, constitutionalism, and liberal policies designed to ensure dissent and free expression. These experiments were not universal, however, and in fact they often flirted with self-destruction. Nevertheless, the United States of America, because of its heritage in Great Britain more than anything else, stood as an example to the world after the defeat of fascism in the 1940s. The watchword was liberty – whatever people understood by the term. America touted itself as the land of the free and a shining city on a hill, diametrically opposed in principle to the totalitarian practices of the Soviet Union and its allies. America (it claimed) tolerated dissent and protected minority rights. It did not require uniform obedience to a unitary authority; in fact, authority had been purposefully divided precisely in order to prevent the kind of mass conformity witnessed in the Eastern bloc, enforced by secret police, show trials, labor camps, and whispers of terror tactics. America had a different story to tell about itself as the last best hope of Western civilization against an alien creed. It stood as a paragon and symbol of a better way.

The extent to which this was, in fact, true is beside the point. The political culture was such that Americans tended to believe that they had an obligation to inspire the world to imitate their freedoms, lest the darkness prevail. At the time, there was evidence that the foreign adversary (i.e., the Russians) had infiltrated the U.S. There was, in fact, a pattern of espionage, subsequently verified and no longer disputed by historians, in response to which the political apparatus set up security measures to halt, frustrate, and expose treason. As it happens, a culture celebrated for its widespread liberties felt enormous pressure to curtail those liberties in pursuit of its security, with the result that the effort swung further and further in some sectors toward a state of hysteria, a panic not unlike the infamous witch trials of Salem. One also can readily see the same dynamics at work in Henrik Ibsen's 1882 play *Enemy of the People* (Miller, 1979). The real-world incident I am writing about was known as the Red Scare. The politician Joseph McCarthy was to capitalize on and intensify this mood. Yet he ultimately failed. Why?

Edward R. Murrow had been a broadcast pioneer during World War II, managing to cover all of Europe as best he could in the days leading up to the outbreak of hostilities, then dutifully reporting live from the rooftops of London during the Blitz.[9] Day after day, Murrow risked death to deliver his sober, concrete, and understated account of what he saw and heard and felt in the smoke-filled, glass-strewn streets and overhead as wave after wave of German bombers soared into the frantic searchlights. Later, once the Allies had gained the upper hand, his nighttime broadcast from inside a bomber over Berlin remains a classic of clinical accuracy, poetic diction, and preternatural calm in the midst of mayhem. For his heroic efforts throughout the war, the American was knighted by Queen Elizabeth, and he received every broadcasting award then in existence, thereby returning to the States after the conflict with immense credibility and routines of professionalism that were to inform his work on both the radio and then television at the CBS.

At CBS, such was Murrow's status that he ignored layers of management and so-called budgets, doing things his way, trading on his reputation for objectivity and independence. Continuously, he resisted interference – not only from his own corporate executives, but also from the government and advertising sponsors. He was a man who supplied his friend Winston Churchill with goods hard

---

9 Three extensive biographies on Murrow include Kendrick, 1969; Sperber, 1986; and Persico, 1988. An excellent place to begin reading about Murrow is Finkelstein, 2005. Another valuable resource about this era is Friendly, 1967/1968.

to obtain in postwar England, and a confidant of Franklin Delano Roosevelt who was in the Oval Office on the night of December 7, 1941. Murrow was even asked to become president of a university (even though he had no faculty experience or advanced academic degree) and to manage the BBC (even though he was an American). He resisted calls to run for the U.S. Senate from the state of New York. Known foremost for his integrity, Murrow had earned an almost Lincolnesque stature with the general public.

Given the context in which he lived, it is important to note that Murrow was not partisan in his politics. He supported in principle America's efforts to repulse the infiltration of its government by foreign agents, and he voluntarily signed a loyalty oath that many of his peers found objectionable. He rejected the doctrines and practices of the Soviet Union, when asked, but his portfolio, so to speak, was on behalf of what were known as liberal precepts, such as due process, the rule of law, fair play, the right to dissent, and constitutionalism.[10] He had witnessed the rise of fascism up close and despised it. He had then toured the concentration camps after the war, which solidified his loathing for everything about fascism's ideology. So, when he insinuated that McCarthyism as a public mood reminded him of fascism, he knew whereof he spoke. He had rejected both Nazism and Bolshevism as creeds because, in his estimation, the ideals of America surpassed them both. With increasing apprehension, therefore, he witnessed the tactics at home of blacklisting, intimidation, and reckless innuendo, championed foremost in the media by the junior senator from Wisconsin.

Senator McCarthy was, in many ways, a product of mass media. He knew how to capture its attention and play on the fears of ordinary folks. He had learned, for example, that the best defense is a good offense, such that anyone who displeased him could suddenly become the object of a congressional inquiry. Or McCarthy would bypass that method and go straight to the audience with assorted, sordid allegations. Distressingly, his popularity led to a kind of reinforcing feedback loop, whereby he slipped further and further toward almost buffoonish thuggery. And when the media was not hanging on his every word, because it made for good copy, it was censoring itself in terror, hoping to evade his wrath. A word from McCarthy could (and sometimes did) ruin a career in broadcasting. And it is important to remember that the government was still trying to figure out its responsibilities of oversight for this newfangled technology, inasmuch as it had to license whoever could take to the airwaves. Broadcasters had reason to worry about what a U.S. senator trailing dozens of vigorous young partisans on Capitol Hill could do to the industry (and its burgeoning profits).

At last, Murrow and his team decided the time had come to expose McCarthy on national television. The method was simple: they would exhibit McCarthy in his own words, contradicting himself, abusing witnesses, and divulging

---

10 Only later did the term "liberal" become shorthand for a left-of-center disposition in American politics. Today, one might call his particular viewpoint "classical liberalism."

to sympathetic audiences his true intent. Except for making a couple of factual corrections, all that Murrow did was comment at the close that whatever one thought about the man McCarthy, the threat had arisen among the American people themselves. They were the ones who sustained the panic. They enabled the demagogue. Is this, he asked, how we like to think of ourselves, resorting to practices that deny liberty on behalf of a creed that we claim is all about the superiority of our way of life?

The response to this broadcast was electric. It is no coincidence that McCarthy's stature diminished quickly, to the point where the Senate itself censured him. Murrow had confronted the menace head on, something barely anyone else had wanted to do. And nobody, except perhaps President Dwight Eisenhower himself, had the moral standing to deliver the blow. Murrow had come forth, but he was not speaking on behalf of a partisan platform or policy proposal or for one political party or the other. Instead, Murrow reached back to founding principles about the rule of law, the right of dissent, free speech, and the liminal arrangement of the Constitution of the United States of America, whereby no single entity could claim complete authority over the lives of its citizens without due process of law. He was calling the people to a prior understanding about what made Americans different from the fascists and the Bolshevists and a dozen tinpot dictators he had scrutinized up close as a reporter.

The obvious thing should not go unsaid: Murrow took a position diametrically opposed to the way Clovis had managed his leadership, especially when the young chieftain had cleaved his warrior in two over a busted vase. I repeat what I said earlier that the lesson is not about the type of leadership. The contexts were entirely different. What Clovis did as a leader would not work in the time of Edward R. Murrow . . . and vice versa. Yet each rose up to establish a standard in the midst of confusing times, drawing the attention of other people. Clovis labored on behalf of a new order when the old one had collapsed. He walked onto the public stage at the end of a long historical process. Murrow labored on behalf of an existing order against those who would destroy it. He stepped in before the forces of disorder could do their worst. Nevertheless, these were both liminal epochs ultimately resolved in part because of the actions of extraordinary leaders.

Comparing one liminal period with another

The philosopher Karl Jaspers (inspired in this by Max Weber) explains that detecting similarities in history is all well and good, but perhaps the more fruitful exercise is detecting differences. When two situations appear to be similar, why then did they turn in completely different directions? If, in the case of Clovis, a disordered society accepted the brutal assertions of the youthful barbarian so that his framework endured more or less for a thousand years, why did the American society threatened with disorder during the Cold War come to itself and reject the blandishments of Joe McCarthy? It will not do to argue that these were very different situations, even though they most certainly were. That is not an explanation. It is a restatement of the question. "They were different because they were different." Not helpful. Instead, the task is to investigate *in what way* they were different. Jaspers (1989) writes, "In similar historical situations, something similar is possible. Hence, in the course of time, the opposite or simply something different occurs" (p. 87).

From this beginning, we might investigate in what way the attempted *leadership* was different, in what way the prospective *followers* were different, in what way the *situation* was different (e.g., legally, economically, religiously). Some differences will of course be less salient. It will not matter, for instance, that they wore different kinds of hats or that they ate different cuts of pork. As Jaspers puts it, "Reality is an infinite weaving of the meaningful and the meaningless" (1989, p. 88). Accordingly, he writes, "Reality is always equally individual in historical, infinite multiplicity" (p. 92). There is no "law" that history obeys. There is barely any generalization or principle.

From such an assertion, one might conclude that there will be nothing of value to obtain from historical research. Of what use would it be to read about episodes that are unlike anything you or I experience today? If everything is different, then nothing can be learned. That sounds like a reasonable inference in light of what Jaspers says. His response to this inference, however, seems to be another question: what did you *expect* to learn?

The antiquarian wants to know what happened, and there's an end to it. History is nothing but a story. But if one wants to learn in order to apply lessons from the past – a past that is inevitably different from the present – to our experiences today, perhaps it would help to reconsider what it is that it would be possible to discover. For, as I have been saying in these pages, one cannot pluck out one lesson from the past and superimpose it today, as though it were a patch of fabric to be sewn over a small hole.[11] History exhibits what is possible. And among the things that are possible is the conceptualization one uses to understand. It is possible to think, to imagine, to infer. What in particular a person believes at any given moment may vary over time, of course – sometimes wildly so. But it is possible to believe certain things about one's predicaments. What people *believe* is crucial to understanding what they *do*.

Here we get to the heart of Jaspers' argument. For in the midst of liminality – that passage through uncertainty, which we might consider to be a crisis, having let go of life's fixities – one grabs for something to believe in, for a reliable guide. When all points of reference disappear, people will go in search of something or someone to help them make sense of their choices. One does not need to verify or validate what in particular that person believes, so much as recognize that folks

11 See generally Ortega, 1940/1946, p. 47.

will latch on to *something*. In those instances, people will cast about looking for somebody who seems to know what to do, whose bravura example indicates in which direction we all might like to go. We are glad, relieved even, to find a person who presumes to show the way. Or at least someone who establishes a framework within which we might figure out the rest.

Clovis established such a rough framework that looked enough like the Roman Empire, as well as Roman Catholicism, to reassure the people living in Late Antiquity (see Voegelin, 1987, p. 26). In my opinion, part of his value lies in the fact that he never offered to solve all the problems that his subjects were facing. He had troubles of his own. But he did understand at some level the importance of framing, of establishing the boundaries – both literal and figurative – that connote a sense of order. Murrow, on the other hand, appealed to an existing framework, calling the public back to its founding, saying in effect that things were not falling apart. We have a legacy, and that legacy is sufficient to rebut the threats that most certainly surround us. The fault lies in abandoning that framework now – for what reputed gain?

No one disputes that one of the primary differences between the two men lies not so much in them as individuals as in the cultural context, made especially vivid in the opening story of the vase of Soissons. In that story, Clovis solidified his status by serving as judge, jury, and executioner of a subordinate, without hope of appeal, abruptly and vindictively smashing his brains in front of the other men. Whatever rights the Frankish knights had claimed under the traditional Germanic law, the king could now ignore with impunity. With Murrow, by way of contrast, the entire controversy against McCarthy was grounded in the rights of individuals to dissent and avoid persecution based on innuendo and unverified suspicions. Nobody may deprive another citizen of these things without due process of impersonal law.

McCarthy had sought to violate the nation's principles for the sake of preserving them. His example, if it had been successful, would have set America adrift on the tides, forsaking one set of principles for a mess of pottage. Murrow had seen what such an experience could lead to. Because of Murrow, the center held. Rather than displacing our beliefs, he reasserted them, gambling (correctly) that the American public would come back to them.[12]

The point, as Jaspers would recognize, is that liminality reveals the extent of contingency in our lives, which in turn makes our adherence to values paramount. Because we live in permanent white water, it is our privilege and duty to make our values plain, almost regardless of what history throws at us. In the teeth

---

12 Sadly, in victory (such as it was) Murrow threw himself into a different controversy that swallowed him whole, namely, the self-indulgent commercialism that was turning television into little more than wires in a box, a steady source of idle amusement. This too had been part of the American ethos. It still is, as anyone with a phone will attest. But that is a challenge for another leader to address . . . and soon.

of vicissitudes, we must decide who we are, come what may. Leadership offers to a people the chance to make those choices, precisely because no two epochs are alike. The people of Late Antiquity made their choices. We make ours. But choose we must, or the radical contingency of life will swamp our little boat and leave us without a trace. I can imagine no greater purpose in studying leadership than designating the ways that humanity struggles to find meaning in life. We do this together, and God bless the ones who show us the way, by their example, their exhortations, and their powers.

In 1933, the Spaniard José Ortega y Gasset delivered a series of lectures on the impact of Galileo on Western thought. Translated and published as a book in English in 1958, the series emphasizes the experience of crisis, a term he uses to depict the acute liminality through which Europe had passed every so many hundreds of years, including of course the fall of the Roman Empire. His description of what we have been calling liminality will sound familiar:

> Man returns to a state of actually not knowing what to think about the world. Therefore the change swells to a crisis and takes on the character of a catastrophe. . . . One does not know what new thing to think – one only knows, or thinks he knows, that the traditional norms and ideas are false and inadmissible. One feels a profound disdain for everything, or almost everything, which was believed yesterday; but the truth is that there are no new positive beliefs with which to replace the traditional ones.
>
> *(p. 86)*

Ortega's conclusion is as follows: "Man adapts himself to everything, to the best and the worst. To one thing only does he not adapt himself: to being not clear in his own mind concerning what he believes about things" (p. 108).

In both the era of Clovis and the era of Murrow, one can recognize the urge to renovate, to get back behind the complexity that seemed to overwhelm the system and begin again, fresh, simple, restoring first principles, without all the excrescences (to borrow Ortega's word) that will have accumulated like so many barnacles on the prevailing culture (1958, p. 217). To some extent, Clovis passed himself off as the new Roman Imperator, putting a violent stop to generations of dislocation, just as Murrow hearkened back to the rule of law protecting the right of dissent, as written into the Declaration of Independence and the Bill of Rights. There was in each of them a backward glance, for whatever it is that emerges in a time of crisis must be found by the people to seem sufficiently reassuring (Voegelin, 1987, p. 26). They must recognize themselves in the newer forms of life. Yet each of these leaders also brought something completely new. Clovis proved to be a harbinger of feudalism and the Middle Ages, blending Germanic mores and Catholicism into the mix. Murrow represented a greater intimacy delivered by novel technology, broadcast worldwide instantaneously.

Ortega credits Galileo with being an initiator, the historical figure who represents the dawn of the modern age (1958, p. 10). Who then was Clovis, if not an initiator? And who then is Murrow? And what sort of age did Murrow initiate – an age through which we are still living in the twenty-first century?

Concluding exhortations

Murrow fit the moment then and in my opinion would fit the moment now, more so than the epoch of Clovis, because our age has experienced forms of democracy and therefore will have expectations that would have been alien to Gaul during Late Antiquity. The man of action putting things to right by extraordinary means, saving the people, should not be necessary. In fact, he (or she) poses a genuine threat to public order. I would say it this way: a people that subordinates itself uncritically to such a paragon thereby squanders its birthright and returns to that extended tutelage which the philosopher Immanuel Kant had warned us about many years ago. In twenty-first century America and to a great extent the West broadly speaking, we should not covet a Clovis, even if many of us yield to the temptation from time to time. What we require instead are more Murrows, characters of vision who call us back to our best selves, invoking our founding principles, without claiming the powers to fix things for us, whether by executive order or martial law. The armature of democracy, consent of the governed, civil liberties, and constitutionalism continue to exist, albeit imperfectly. As I look around, I am unaware of any viable alternative to the basic principles prevailing in the West today. Even if, as many suggest, people should take to the streets in order to dismantle existing institutions, they have no ideology, no articulation of principles by which the public might wish to be governed and which convinces many to shut down dissent altogether and eviscerate the protection of free speech. If your political agenda cannot successfully compete for acceptance, for whatever reason, then the seductive alternative remedy is to silence others.[13]

At some risk, therefore, I do make the provocative claim that McCarthyism is among us still, albeit in a different guise.

It has been a recurring theme in my book that the collapse of the Roman Empire established the bewildering conditions within which a Clovis was able to operate. And what a relief it was for Gaul to find itself again at peace. But things today are indeed different. The order has not collapsed. And there is as yet no viable alternative belief system. Charismatic leaders we have a-plenty, although most of them find mere celebrity more attractive than politics. The leadership we require, so far as I can tell (and indeed I am editorializing), is equivalent to Murrow's, warning us against the feverish, the panic-driven, the nihilistic, and the craven. Perhaps, like Murrow, we have more to fear from our obsession with

---

13 For an extended critique of this emerging mindset in the twenty-first century, see Rauch, 2021.

amusement and commercial gain than we do from traitors or rebels in our midst. For if the order does collapse – and one day, it assuredly will – it will have been our fault, collectively. If I had a parting wish then for my reader, it is this: let us live so that we need no Clovis, ruthless and grim, to pick up the pieces of a disintegrating world.

References

Ando, C. (2008, Spring). "Decline, fall, and transformation." *Journal of Late Antiquity*. 1(1): 31–60.

Bileta, V. (2016). "The last legions: The 'barbarization' of military identity in the Late Roman West." *Tabula: časopis Filozofskog fakulteta, Sveučilište Jurja Dobrile u Puli*. (14): 22–42.

Carlyle, T. (1902). *On heroes, hero worship, and the heroic in history*. Ginn & Co.

Derrida, J. (1978). "Structure, sign and play in the discourse of the human sciences." In Derrida, J. (ed.). *Writing and difference* (ch. 10, A. Bass, trans.). University of Chicago Press.

Dobry, M. (2015). "Critical processes and political fluidity." In Horvath, A., Thomassen, B. & H. Wydra (eds.). *Breaking boundaries: Varieties of liminality* (ch. 5). Berghahn.

Finkelstein, N. (2005). *With heroic truth: The life of Edward R. Murrow*. Authors Guild Backinprint.com.

Foucault, M. (1997). *"Society must be defended": Lectures at the College de France, 1975–76* (D. Macey, trans.). Picador.

Fouracre, P. (2020a). "Feudal revolution? Transformations around the year 1000." In Mossman, S. (ed.). *Debating Medieval Europe: The early Middle Ages, c. 450–c.1050* (ch. 5). Manchester University Press.

Fouracre, P. (2020b). "The successor states, 550–750." In Mossman, S. (ed.). *Debating Medieval Europe: The early Middle Ages, c. 450-c.1050* (ch. 2). Manchester University Press.

Fouracre, P. (2022). "From Gaul to Francia: The impact of the Merovingians." In Effros, B. & Moreira, I. (eds.). *The Oxford handbook of the Merovingian world* (ch. 2). Oxford University Press.

Friendly, F. (1967/1968). *Due to circumstances beyond our control . . ..* Vintage Books.

Giessen, B. (2015). "Inbetweenness and ambivalence." In Horvath, A., Thomassen, B. & Wydra, H. (eds.). *Breaking boundaries: Varieties of liminality* (ch. 3). Berghahn.

Girard, R. (1989). *The scapegoat*. Johns Hopkins University Press.

Haun, J. (2013, May). "A new system of power: The Franks and the Catholic church in post-Roman Gaul." (Doctoral dissertation. University of Texas at Arlington).

Horvath, A. (2020). "Beyond charisma: Catacombing sensual governance by painful breaking of human ties." In Horvath, A., Szakolczai, A. & Marangudakis, M. (eds.). *Modern leaders: Between charisma and trickery* (ch. 1). Routledge.

Horvath, A. (2015). "The genealogy of political alchemy." In Horvath, A., Thomassen, B. & Wydra, H. (eds.). *Breaking boundaries: Varieties of liminality* (ch. 4). Berghahn.

Horvath, A., Szakolczai, A. & Marangudakis, M. (2020). "Introduction." In Horvath, A., Szakolczai, A. & Marangudakis, M. (eds.). *Modern leaders: Between charisma and trickery* (pp. 1–11). Routledge.

Horvath, A., Thomassen, B. & Wydra, H. (2015). "Introduction." In Horvath, A., Thomassen, B. & Wydra, H. (eds.). *Breaking boundaries: Varieties of liminality* (pp. 1–8). Berghahn.

Jaspers, K. (1989). *On Max Weber* (R. Whelan, trans.). Paragon House.

Kendrick, A. (1969). *Prime time: The life of Edward R. Murrow*. Avon Publishers.

Mathisen, R. (2019). "The end of the western Roman Empire in the fifth century CE: Barbarian auxiliaries, independent military contractors, and civil wars." In Drijvers, J. & Lenski, N. (eds.). *The fifth century: Age of transformation* (pp. 137–156) [Proceedings of the 12th Biennial Shifting Frontiers in Late Antiquity conference]. Edipuglia.

Miller, A. (1979). *Arthur Miller's adaptation of "An Enemy of the People"*. Penguin Group.

Nelson, J. (2020). "The Carolingian moment." In Mossman, S. (ed.). *Debating Medieval Europe: The early Middle Ages, c. 450–c.1050* (ch. 3). Manchester University Press.

Ortega y Gasset, J. (1958). *Man and crisis* (M. Adams, trans.). W. W. Norton & Co.

Ortega y Gasset, J. (1940/1946). *Concord and liberty* (H. Weyl, trans.). W. W. Norton & Co.

Persico, J. (1988). *Edward R. Murrow: An American original*. McGraw-Hill.

Peterson, M.A. (2015). "In search of anti-structure." In Horvath, A., Thomassen, B. & Wydra, H. (eds.). *Breaking boundaries: Varieties of liminality* (ch. 9). Berghahn.

Potter, D. (2021). *Disruption: Why things change*. Oxford University Press.

Rauch, J. (2021). *The constitution of knowledge: A defense of truth*. Brookings Institution Press.

Roman, C.F. (2015). "Liminality, the execution of Louis XVI, and the rise of terror during the French Revolution." In Horvath, A., Thomassen, B. & Wydra, H. (eds.). *Breaking boundaries: Varieties of liminality* (ch. 8). Berghahn.

Solzhenitsyn, A. (1984–1991). *The red wheel*. Farrar, Straus and Giroux and University of Notre Dame Press.

Sperber, A.M. (1986). *Murrow: His life and times*. Freundlich Books.

Szakolczai, A. (2015). "Liminality and experience." In Horvath, A., Thomassen, B. & Wydra, H. (eds.). *Breaking boundaries: Varieties of liminality* (ch. 1). Berghahn.

Thomassen, B. (2015). "Thinking with liminality." In Horvath, A., Thomassen, B. & Wydra, H. (eds.). *Breaking boundaries: Varieties of liminality* (ch. 2). Berghahn.

Voegelin, E. (1987). *Order and history: In search of order* (vol. 5). Louisiana State University Press.

Ward-Perkins, B. (2005). *The fall of Rome and the end of civilization*. Oxford University Press.

APPENDIX 1

Map

Reference

Wasson, D.L. (2014, November 10). "Clovis I." *Ancient History Encyclopedia*. Retrieved 16 September 2020 from www.ancient.eu/Clovis_I/.

APPENDIX 2

Time line[1]

- c. 466 BCE: Clovis is born
- c. 481: Clovis's father, Childeric I, dies and is succeeded by Clovis (reign begins)
- c. 486: Clovis defeats Syagrius in Soissons and begins the takeover of the kingdom
- c. 491: Clovis completes the conquest of the kingdom
- c. 493:

  Clovis agrees to marriage of his sister Audofleda to Theodoric the Great
  Clovis marries a Burgundian princess, Clotilde

- c. 496:

  Clovis is baptized (early estimate)
  Clovis defeats the Alamanni threat

- c. 500: Clovis subjugates Burgundy
- c. 507: Battle of Vouillé, where Clovis defeats Alaric II of the Visigoths
- c. 508: Clovis baptized by the Bishop of Reims (late estimate)
- c. 509: Clovis is declared the king of all the Franks
- 511

  First Council of Orléans
  November 27 (or 513): Clovis dies in Paris

Reference

Pestano, D. (2015–16). "Clovis, king of the Franks: Towards a new chronology (9 parts)." *Dark Age History*. Retrieved 16 September 2020 from https://darkagehistory.blogspot.com/2015/06/clovisking-of-frankstowards-new_9.html.

---

1 Most of these dates are contested (see, e.g., Pestano, 2015–16).

INDEX

Printed in the United States
by Baker & Taylor Publisher Services